NODE.JS
IN A NUTSHELL

A Practical Guide
To Master Node.js

David Mark

Table of Contents

Introduction

In this introductory lesson, we'll learn what Node.js is and why you might want to learn it. If you visit nodejs.org, the official website for Node.js, you'll see it described as an "open-source, cross-platform JavaScript runtime environment." Let's break this down:

- **Open-source:** This means the source code for Node.js is publicly available for everyone to share and modify.
- **Cross-platform:** It's available for Mac, Windows, and Linux, making it incredibly versatile.
- **JavaScript runtime environment:** To understand this, we need to take a step back and learn what a JavaScript runtime environment is. We'll explore this in detail later in the book.

For now, let me give you some compelling reasons why you might want to learn Node.js:

- **Build End-to-End JavaScript Applications:** Node.js allows you to create full-stack applications using just JavaScript. That means you can develop both the front-end (what users see) and the back-end (the server-side logic) using the same language.
- **Used by Major Companies:** Many big names like LinkedIn, Netflix, and PayPal have adopted Node.js as their backend technology. This shows its reliability and performance.
- **In-Demand Skill:** Full-stack development is a highly sought-after skillset. Learning Node.js can help you land your dream job, especially if you're already a front-end developer.
- **Large Community Support:** There's a huge community behind Node.js, which means you'll have plenty of resources and support if you encounter any issues.

Remember, this book focuses on the core concepts of Node.js. While you'll be able to build basic applications, frameworks like Express.js are essential for building complex web applications.

The only prerequisite for this book is modern JavaScript. If you're new to JavaScript, please check out my books on JavaScript.

ECMAScript

In this lesson, we'll dive into a crucial concept called **ECMAScript**, which forms the bedrock of JavaScript. So, let's journey back in time! Imagine a world without dynamic web pages – only static content, no interactivity. This was the reality in 1993 when the first web browser with a user interface, **Mosaic**, was released. The Mosaic developers went on to establish **Netscape** and brought us **Netscape Navigator** – a more polished browser that quickly gained popularity.

But, there was a problem – the web pages were static. There was no way to add dynamic behavior after a page loaded. This meant no interactive elements, no user-specific content updates, no engaging user experiences! To solve this, in 1995, Netscape introduced a new scripting language called **JavaScript**. They cleverly named it JavaScript to ride the wave of **Java's** popularity at that time.

Around the same time, **Microsoft** launched its browser, **Internet Explorer**. This sparked a browser war, with each striving to be the best. Microsoft recognized JavaScript's potential to transform the web experience and wanted a similar scripting language for Internet Explorer. However, they had no official specification to follow. To catch up, Microsoft reverse-engineered Netscape Navigator's interpreter in 1996 and created their own scripting language called **JScript**. JScript filled the same use case as JavaScript but differed in its implementation.

This led to a significant problem. The differences between JavaScript and JScript made it difficult for developers to create websites that worked well in both browsers. Imagine the frustration of having your website look great on Netscape but break on Internet Explorer, or vice versa! To combat this, Netscape submitted JavaScript to **ECMA International** in November 1996.

Now, you might be wondering, "What's ECMA International?". It's an organization that sets standards for information and communication systems. Netscape wanted a standard specification for JavaScript that all browser vendors could adhere to, ensuring consistent implementations across browsers.

For every new specification, ECMA provides a standard specification and a committee. For JavaScript, the standard is called **ECMA-262**, and the committee working on it is called **Technical Committee 39**, or **TC39** for short.

ECMA decided to use the term **ECMAScript** for the official language, as Oracle, who acquired Microsystems, owned the trademark for "JavaScript". So, ECMAScript is the standard, while JavaScript is the language we actually use in practice, built upon that standard.

Over the years, we've had many versions of ECMAScript released. **ES2015**, also known as **ES6**, is the version that introduced "modern JavaScript features" and is a must-know for modern JavaScript development.

Now, here's a twist! Although ECMAScript and JavaScript are technically distinct, they're often used interchangeably. For our purposes in this book, it won't make a huge difference. When you encounter "ECMAScript", think of it as JavaScript.

To summarize, **ECMA-262** is the language specification, **ECMAScript** is the language implementing ECMA-262, and **JavaScript** is essentially ECMAScript at its core with additional features. For our journey, we can safely consider ECMAScript as JavaScript, the language we're all familiar with!

In the next lesson, we'll explore the **Chrome V8 engine**, the engine behind Node.js, which is powered by ECMAScript (or, as we'll call it, JavaScript). Get ready to dive into the engine room!

Chrome's V8 Engine

In this lesson, we're diving into the heart of Node.js - the V8 engine. Think of it like the engine of a car: it's what makes things run. But instead of powering a car, V8 powers your JavaScript code.

We know computers don't understand JavaScript code directly. They need something called a **JavaScript engine**. A JavaScript engine is like a translator. It takes the code we write (JavaScript) and converts it into something the computer can understand (machine code). Think of it as translating from English to French!

There are several JavaScript engines out there, like **SpiderMonkey** for Firefox, **JavaScriptCore** for Safari, and **Chakra** for the original Microsoft Edge. But the one we're interested in is **V8**.

V8 is Google's open-source JavaScript engine, and it's the backbone of Chrome and Node.js. Head over to v8.dev. You'll find tons of information about V8. Click on "Docs" and scroll down to "Checking out the V8 source code". Click on the GitHub repo link.

Take a look at the README lesson. There are a few key points to understand:

- **V8 is Google's open-source JavaScript engine.** We already know what a JavaScript engine does, so this makes sense!
- **V8 implements ECMAScript as specified in ECMA-262.** Remember that ECMAScript is the standard language specification for JavaScript. V8 follows these rules to make sure our JavaScript code behaves the same way across different browsers and platforms.
- **V8 is written in C++ and is used in Google Chrome.** This is a bit surprising! It means the engine itself isn't written in JavaScript, but in C++. C++ is a more powerful language for certain tasks, like managing memory and interacting with the computer's hardware.
- **V8 can run standalone or can be embedded into any C++ application.** This is where Node.js comes in!

Think of it like this: V8 is a powerful engine, and we can use it independently to execute JavaScript. But we can also embed it into our own C++ programs. This allows us to add features to JavaScript that aren't available in the standard language! That's exactly what Node.js does.

Node.js is essentially a C++ program with V8 embedded in it. This allows Node.js to access the powerful features of V8, and even extend JavaScript with features from C++, like working with files, databases, and networking.

JavaScript Runtime

Let's talk about JavaScript Runtime. It's the secret sauce that makes our JavaScript code come alive. Think of it as the kitchen where your JavaScript recipe gets cooked.

You might already know that every browser has a built-in JavaScript engine. The engine is like the chef who understands the recipe and gets things done. But there's more to it than just the chef! The whole kitchen needs to be equipped with all the right tools and ingredients. That's where the JavaScript Runtime comes in.

Let's take Chrome as an example. When you write JavaScript code in Chrome, it gets executed in Chrome's JavaScript Runtime. It's like a well-organized kitchen with all the necessary tools. Here's what's inside:

The JavaScript Engine (V8): This is the heart of the operation. The V8 engine, like our chef, understands the JavaScript code and executes it. It has a special area called the **Call Stack** where your code gets processed step by step. It also has a **Heap** – a storage area for all the ingredients, or variables, that your JavaScript application needs.

Web APIs: Think of these as the fancy kitchen appliances. They add extra functionality beyond the basic JavaScript language. Examples include:

- `setTimeout` **and** `setInterval`**:** These let you schedule tasks to happen later. Like setting a timer!
- **Promises:** These help you deal with asynchronous tasks – things that happen in the background.
- **Browser Storage:** This allows your application to store data locally in the browser.

- **Queues:** Imagine a waiting area where asynchronous tasks patiently wait their turn. These are queues, and they hold tasks that need to be completed in a specific order.

- **Event Loop:** Finally, we have the event loop. It's like the manager who makes sure everything runs smoothly. It checks the queues, moves tasks to the call stack when they're ready, and makes sure the engine is busy doing useful work.

So, the JavaScript Runtime is more than just the engine. It's the complete environment that makes JavaScript work. Without all these components, our code wouldn't run.

Think of it this way:

- **ECMAScript:** The recipe itself.
- **JavaScript Engine:** The chef who understands the recipe and can cook it.
- **JavaScript Runtime:** The entire kitchen with all the tools and appliances needed to execute the recipe.

Now, we understand that just a JavaScript engine isn't enough. A browser needs a complete JavaScript Runtime to run the JavaScript code we write every day.

What is Node.js?

Remember how we talked about JavaScript runtimes in the last lesson? Well, now it's time to dive deeper into Node.js itself!

We already know a few things about Node.js:

- **Open Source:** Anyone can see and change the code, making it super collaborative.
- **Cross-Platform:** It works on Mac, Windows, and Linux. Pretty versatile, right?

Now, with our understanding of runtimes, we can add another piece to the puzzle: Node.js is a **JavaScript runtime environment**. It's like a big toolbox that contains everything you need to run JavaScript programs. The really cool part is that **Node.js lets you run JavaScript outside of a web browser**.

Before Node.js came along in 2009, JavaScript was pretty much stuck inside the browser. But with Node.js, we can do **so much more**!

- **Websites:** Traditional websites, just like the ones you use every day.
- **Back-end Services (APIs):** The invisible code that makes websites work, like fetching data from a database or sending you notifications.
- **Real-time Applications:** Things like live chat or online games, where things update instantly.
- **Streaming Services:** You can use Node.js to build streaming services like Netflix, where you can watch lessons and movies.
- **Command Line Tools:** Those programs you use in your terminal window to do things like manage files or build software.
- **Multiplayer Games:** You can create multiplayer games using Node.js, so you can play with your friends online.

Node.js gives you the power to create **complex and powerful applications**.

Let's get a little bit technical and analyze the Node.js runtime. We'll take a peek at its source code and see how it works.

- **GitHub:** The source code for Node.js is available on GitHub. You can find it at https://github.com/nodejs/node.

- **Dependencies Folder:** This folder holds all the external code that Node.js relies on. Two really important dependencies are:
  - **V8:** The same JavaScript engine used in the Chrome browser. It's what allows Node.js to understand the JavaScript code you write.
  - **libuv:** An open-source library that helps Node.js interact with the operating system, giving it access to things like files and networks.
- **Source Folder:** This folder contains the C++ source code for the Node.js runtime. Remember, JavaScript wasn't designed for low-level tasks like interacting with the file system or network. C++ was, so Node.js uses C++ to handle those things.

- **Lib Folder:** This is where Node.js provides JavaScript code that gives you easy access to the C++ features. For example, the `fs.js` file contains code for working with the file system. You can write simple JavaScript code to access files and the `fs.js` file will take care of talking to the C++ code, which then uses libuv to interact with the operating system.

So, Node.js isn't a big, mysterious black box. It's just a bunch of code written in C++ and JavaScript, working together to make your JavaScript code run outside the browser.

A Key Difference: One thing to remember is that the Node.js runtime **doesn't have access to the web APIs** that you use in the browser. There's no `window` or `document` object in Node.js.

Let's recap what we learned:
- **Node.js is a JavaScript runtime environment:** It's the software that allows you to run JavaScript code outside of a browser.
- **It's open source and cross-platform:** Anyone can contribute, and it works on many different operating systems.

- **It's not a language or a framework:** It's the foundation on which you build your JavaScript applications.
- **It's powered by V8 and libuv:** These are crucial components that make Node.js work.
- **It provides access to C++ features:** Node.js lets you use low-level features through JavaScript code.

We've covered a lot of ground about Node.js. Now it's time to put it all into practice. In the next lesson, we'll finally write our first Node.js program.

Hello World

"Node.js" is often just called "Node". We'll be using that shorter term throughout our journey. Let's set up your development environment and write our first "Hello World" program with Node.

First, you need an editor. I prefer VS Code, which is a popular choice and free! You can grab it from code.visualstudio.com.

Next up, you need Node.js itself. There are a bunch of ways to install Node depending on your computer (Windows, Mac, Linux), but the easiest route is to head over to nodejs.org. Download the latest version (as of this writing, it's 19.1.0). Run the installer, stick with the default settings, and you're good to go.

Alright, let's put VS Code to work. Create a new folder on your computer for our Node.js projects. Open VS Code and open this folder.

Open the integrated terminal in VS Code. You can find it under the "View" menu, select "Terminal," or use the shortcut `Ctrl+` (backtick).

In the terminal, type `node -v` and press Enter. If you see the version of Node you just installed, you're ready to roll! If you get an error, double-check your installation or search online for the error message.

Now, it's time to learn how to execute JavaScript code with Node. There are two methods, let's explore both:

Method 1: Node REPL

REPL stands for "Read Evaluate Print Loop". It's like a super-fast calculator for JavaScript. In the terminal, type `clear` and press Enter to clear the screen. Next, type `node` and press Enter. This opens an interactive shell where you can execute Node.js code.

Let's try this:

```
console.log("Hello World!");
```

Press Enter. You'll see "Hello World!" printed in the terminal, followed by `undefined`, which is the return value of the `console.log` statement.

Now, let's try a simple math problem:

```
2 + 2;
```

Press Enter. You'll see the result, `4`, printed in the terminal.

So, the Node REPL reads your JavaScript code, evaluates it, prints the result, and loops back to wait for your next command. You can quit the REPL by pressing `Ctrl + D`.

Method 2: Running JavaScript Code from a File

While REPL is cool, the preferred method for building applications is to write your JavaScript code in a file and run it using the `node` command.

In VS Code, create a new file in your `project folder` and name it `index.js` (you can also use `app.js`, `main.js`, or any name you like).

Inside the file, type this:

```
console.log("Hello from index.js");
```

Save the file.

Back in the terminal, run the following command:

```
node index.js
```

Press Enter. You'll see "Hello from index.js" printed in the terminal! That's it! You just ran your first Node.js program!

We've successfully installed Node.js, verified our installation, and learned about two ways to run JavaScript code with Node:

- **Node REPL**: A great tool for quick testing and experimentation.
- **Running code from a file**: The preferred way for building applications.

Now you're ready to start writing some amazing Node.js applications!

Browser vs Node.js

Remember in the last lesson we learned how to run JavaScript code using Node.js. We even executed JavaScript code outside the browser! But even though it's JavaScript, there are some important differences between how it works in the browser and in Node.js.

Think of it like this: Imagine you have a friend who loves to bake cookies. They can use the same ingredients in the kitchen (JavaScript), but they might make different treats depending on what tools they have available.

In the browser, most of the time we're interacting with the **DOM (Document Object Model)**. This is like a recipe for how the webpage looks and behaves. We use things like `document`, `window`, and `cookies` to make changes to the webpage.

But Node.js doesn't have a DOM! It's not designed to manipulate web pages. Instead, it's like a kitchen with tools for different tasks, like accessing the file system or making requests to other servers. It has lots of **modules** that provide these tools, like the `fs` module for working with files.

Here's another difference: In Node.js, you're the chef! You control the environment and choose which version of Node.js your application runs on. That means you can use all the latest and greatest JavaScript features, like **ES6**, **ES7**, **ES8**, and **ES9**.

But in the browser, it's like using a public oven. You don't get to decide what version of the oven is available. If a user is using an old browser, you might have to work around limitations.

Let's see an example:

```
// Browser JavaScript
```

```
console.log(document.getElementById('myButton')); //
Accessing the DOM

// Node.js JavaScript
const fs = require('fs');
fs.readFile('myfile.txt', (err, data) => {
  if (err) {
    console.error(err);
  } else {
    console.log(data.toString());
  }
}); // Reading a file from the file system
```

This is important to remember: When writing JavaScript, keep in mind if you're working in the browser or in Node.js. They have different strengths and weaknesses! Try to run the above code with node.

So, what's next? We've learned a lot about JavaScript, its runtime environments, and the basics of Node.js. Now, let's dive into the world of **modules** in Node.js. Modules are like specialized ingredients that give Node.js its power. Stay tuned for our next lesson!

Watch Mode

It's a neat feature in Node.js version 18 and above. This mode automatically restarts your Node.js process whenever you make changes to the code. It's a real time-saver when you're constantly updating files and checking the output!

Let's add a simple `console.log` statement in our `index.js` file:
```
console.log("Hello world");
```

Normally, we'd have to run `node index.js` again each time we change this file. But with watch mode, we can simply run this command in our terminal:
```
node --watch index.js
```

This will print the output, and any changes you make to the `index.js` file will trigger a restart, allowing you to see the updated output.

If you change the `console.log` statement to `console.log("Hello David")` and save the file, you'll see the output update immediately.

Modules

Think of a module as a little package of code that does a specific job. It's like a reusable toolbox you can grab whenever you need it.

Node.js has a few different kinds of modules. We'll explore them all, but for now, let's focus on the ones we can create ourselves, called **local modules**.

Imagine you're building a house. You might have separate workers for the plumbing, the electrical wiring, and the framing. Each worker has their own set of tools and knowledge, just like modules! We use local modules to organize our code and make it easier to manage large projects.

Let's break it down:

What is a local module?

It's a JavaScript file we write that contains functions, variables, or other code we want to reuse in our project.

How do we create one?

It's as simple as creating a new JavaScript file! For example, let's say we want to make a module called greeting.js that will provide a simple function to greet someone.

Code Example:

```
// greeting.js
function greet(name) {
  console.log(`Hello, ${name}!`);
}

module.exports = { greet };
```

In this example, we have a function called greet that takes a name as an input and prints a greeting to the console. Notice the line module.exports = { greet }; This tells Node.js that we want to make the greet function accessible from other parts of our application.

How do we use our module?

Let's create a new file, main.js, to use the module we just created:

Code Example:

```
// main.js
const greetings = require('./greeting.js');
greetings.greet("Alice");
```

Explanation:

- `const greetings = require('./greeting.js');`: This line imports the `greeting.js` module. The `require` function tells Node.js to load the file and make its contents available.
- `greetings.greet("Alice");`: Now we can use the `greet` function from our `greetings.js` module. We call it with the name "Alice" as input.

Output:

```
Hello, Alice!
```

Local Modules

Let's start with a simple example. We have our `index.js` file, which currently just logs "Hello from index.js" to the console. We'll add a function to calculate the sum of two numbers within this file.

```
// index.js
console.log("Hello from index.js");

const add = (a, b) => a + b;

const sum = add(1, 2);
console.log(sum);
```

If we run `node index.js`, we see both "Hello from index.js" and "3" printed in the terminal. This works, but as your project grows, it's best to keep related code organized in separate modules. Think of it like separating your Lego pieces into different containers - much easier to manage, right?

Let's create a new file called `add.js` in the same folder as `index.js`. This will become our first module. We'll move the `add` function and its usage to `add.js`.

```
// add.js
const add = (a, b) => a + b;

const sum = add(1, 2);
```

```
console.log(sum);
```

Now, if you run `node index.js` again, you'll only see "Hello from index.js". Why? Because Node.js treats each file as an isolated module. Even if we add some incorrect JavaScript code to `add.js`, `index.js` still runs without errors.

To include our `add.js` module in `index.js`, we use the `require` function, a powerful tool that comes built-in with Node.js.

```
// index.js

const add = require('./add'); // Import and execute the add module

console.log("Hello from index.js");
```

Now, if you run `node index.js`, you'll see the output as before: "3" followed by "Hello from index.js". This is because the `require` function loads the `add.js` module into `index.js`, executes the code in `add.js`, and then continues with the rest of the code in `index.js`.

One more thing: You can omit the `.js` extension when using `require` for JavaScript files. Node.js will automatically append it and try to load the module.

In the next lesson, we'll learn how to expose specific functionality from a module while keeping the rest private, allowing for controlled code sharing between modules.

Exports

In the previous lesson, we learned how to load a module using the `require` function. By requiring a module, we essentially tell V8 (Node.js's JavaScript engine) to execute the code in that module. While this works, the real power of modules comes in when we want to share and reuse code across different parts of our application. This is where the magic of `module.exports` comes in!

Let's say we have a file called `add.js` which contains a simple function to add two numbers:

```
// add.js
```

```
function add(a, b) {
   return a + b;
}
```

Instead of directly calling add and logging the sum within add.js, we want to make this function accessible to other files. To do this, we assign the add function to the special module.exports object:

```
// add.js
function add(a, b) {
   return a + b;
}

module.exports = add;
```

So, what's so special about module.exports? Well, the value assigned to module.exports is exactly what the require function returns for that module. This means we can now use our add function in another file like this:

```
// index.js
const add = require('./add'); // './' tells Node.js to
look for the file in the same directory

const sum = add(1, 2);
console.log(sum);
```

Now, when you run node index.js in your terminal, you'll see the output 3 printed to the console. The beauty of this approach is that we can reuse our add function as many times as we want! We could even calculate another sum:

```
// index.js
const add = require('./add');

const sum = add(1, 2);
console.log(sum);

const sum2 = add(2, 3);
console.log(sum2);
```

Running this code will print both 3 and 5 to the console.

A key point to remember is that when we use require to get the value from module.exports, the variable name we use can be anything. Instead of add, we could have used addFunction, and as long as we update our function calls accordingly, we'd get the same result. This is called a "default export".

Modules are fundamental to Node.js. They allow us to create reusable code blocks and organize our projects efficiently. By using `module.exports` and `require`, we can import functions, objects, or even entire modules from other files. This approach, known as the CommonJS format, is a cornerstone of Node.js development.

Exercise:

Let's create a new file called `subtract.js` and write a function to subtract two numbers. Then, use `module.exports` to export the `subtract` function and import it into `index.js` to calculate the difference between two numbers.

Solution:

```
// subtract.js
function subtract(a, b) {
   return a - b;
}

module.exports = subtract;
// index.js
const subtract = require('./subtract');

const difference = subtract(5, 2);
console.log(difference); // Output: 3
```

Exercise:

Create a new module called `calculator.js` that has functions for basic arithmetic operations (addition, subtraction, multiplication, division). Write a `main.js` file to use your `calculator.js` module.

Solution:

calculator.js:

```
function add(a, b) {
   return a + b;
}

function subtract(a, b) {
   return a - b;
}

function multiply(a, b) {
```

```
    return a * b;
}

function divide(a, b) {
  if (b === 0) {
    return "Division by zero is not allowed!";
  } else {
    return a / b;
  }
}

module.exports = { add, subtract, multiply, divide };
```

main.js:

```
const calculator = require('./calculator.js');

let num1 = 5;
let num2 = 3;

console.log(`Addition: ${calculator.add(num1, num2)}`);
console.log(`Subtraction: ${calculator.subtract(num1,
num2)}`);
console.log(`Multiplication: ${calculator.multiply(num1,
num2)}`);
console.log(`Division: ${calculator.divide(num1,
num2)}`);
```

See? We can create them, reuse them, and combine them to build bigger and more complex applications.

As you continue to learn more about Node.js, you'll discover even more ways to use modules effectively. We'll explore these concepts in greater detail in the upcoming lessons.

Scope

Let's start by creating two new modules. We'll call them batman.js and superman.js.

Inside batman.js**:**

```
const superhero = 'Batman';
console.log(superhero);
```

Inside superman.js**:**

```
const superhero = 'Superman';
```

```
console.log(superhero);
```

Now, let's create a file called `index.js` to connect these superheroes.

Inside `index.js`:

```
require('./batman.js');
require('./superman.js');
```

This `require` function is like inviting our superheroes to our team. We're importing the `batman.js` and `superman.js` modules.

If we run `node index.js` in our terminal, what do you think will be logged to the console?

...

You'll see the output:

```
Batman
Superman
```

The cool thing is that both superheroes can share the same variable name (`superhero`) without any conflicts. Why? Because each module in Node.js has its own **scope**.

Imagine you have a special box for each superhero. They can't access the contents of another superhero's box, and their actions within their own box don't affect other boxes. This is how modules work!

Node.js uses something called **Immediately Invoked Function Expressions (IIFEs)** to achieve this magic. Let's break it down with an example.

Create a new file called `ife.js`:

```
(function() {
  const superhero = 'Batman';
  console.log(superhero);
})();

(function() {
  const superhero = 'Superman';
  console.log(superhero);
})();
```

This code might look a bit complicated, but let me explain. We're creating two functions wrapped in parentheses (`()`) to make them function expressions. Then, we add another pair of parentheses at the end (), which immediately invokes the function.

Each IIFE creates its own private space (like the special box for our superheroes) where variables and functions can live without affecting anything outside.

Under the hood, Node.js uses a similar IIFE pattern for modules. When you load a module, Node.js wraps the module's code inside an IIFE, providing it with its own private scope. This prevents any conflicts when you import multiple modules.

Advantages of Module Scope:
- **No Conflicts:** You can use the same variable names or function names in different modules without worrying about them stepping on each other's toes.
- **Encapsulation:** Modules keep their internal workings private, which makes your code more organized and manageable.
- **Reusability:** You can easily reuse modules in different parts of your application without worrying about side effects.

Exercise:

Try creating two modules that calculate the area of a rectangle and a triangle, respectively. Make sure both modules use a variable named result to store the calculated area. Use console.log to print the results in the index.js file. Can you do it without any errors?

Solution:

rectangle.js:
```
function calculateRectangleArea(length, width) {
  const result = length * width;
  console.log("Rectangle Area:", result);
}

calculateRectangleArea(5, 3);
```

triangle.js:
```
function calculateTriangleArea(base, height) {
  const result = 0.5 * base * height;
  console.log("Triangle Area:", result);
}
```

```
calculateTriangleArea(4, 6);
```

index.js:
```
require('./rectangle.js');
require('./triangle.js');
```

This code will work without any conflicts because each module has its own private scope.

Wrapper

In the last lesson, we learned that every module in Node.js is wrapped in a special function before it's loaded. This helps keep variables within a module's scope, preventing them from cluttering the global object. But the fun part is, this function comes with five special parameters that play a crucial role in how Node.js manages modules. Let's dive in!

To understand how these parameters work, let's first look at a simple example. Imagine you have a file called `iffy.js` with two functions.

```
// iffy.js
(function(message) {
  console.log(message + " Batman");
})("Hello");

(function(message) {
  console.log(message + " Superman");
})("Hey");
```

These are Immediately Invoked Function Expressions (IIFE), which means they are executed as soon as they are defined. We can pass arguments to them like "Hello" and "Hey." Running `node iffy.js` will output:

```
Hello Batman
Hey Superman
```

Now let's go back to Node.js modules. Here's a simple module:

```
// module.js
const superhero = "Batman";
console.log(superhero);
```

This code defines a variable `superhero` and logs it to the console. Node.js, however, wraps this code within an IIFE, like this:

```
// module.js (after wrapping)
(function(exports, require, module, __filename,
```

```
__dirname) {
  const superhero = "Batman";
  console.log(superhero);
})(exports, require, module, __filename, __dirname);
```

See those five parameters? They are what make modules work their magic.

Let's break down these parameters:

- `exports`: This parameter is the central hub for exporting values from your module. We'll explore this more in detail later.

- `require`: You already know this one! It's the function that lets you import other modules.

- `module`: This parameter represents the current module itself. You can access its properties like the file name and exported values.

- `__filename`: A string representing the absolute path to the current file. For example, if the file is `myModule.js`, it will contain something like `/Users/yourname/Documents/nodeProject/myModule.js`.

- `__dirname`: A string representing the absolute path to the directory where the current file is located. Using the previous example, this would be `/Users/yourname/Documents/nodeProject`.

The best way to understand these parameters is to see them in action. Open your debugger in Node.js and place a breakpoint at the beginning of your module code. When you run the code, you'll see these parameters in the debug panel.

To see how these parameters change when you import other modules, step through the execution. You'll notice that `__filename` and `__dirname` update accordingly based on the file you are currently executing.

So, remember, when you write a Node.js module, it's actually wrapped in an IIFE with these five parameters. They provide the tools you need to import other modules, export your own values, and access information about the current module itself. This structure allows Node.js to manage modules efficiently and avoid conflicts in the global namespace.

Caching

In our last two lessons, we learned about module scope and the module wrapper. Now, we're diving into another crucial concept: module caching. To understand how this works, let's create a new file named `superhero.js`.

```
class Superhero {
  constructor(name) {
    this.name = name;
  }

  getName() {
    return this.name;
  }

  setName(name) {
    this.name = name;
  }
}

module.exports = new Superhero('Batman');
```

This file defines a `Superhero` class with a constructor, a `getName` method, and a `setName` method. We also export an instance of this class with the name 'Batman'.

Now, let's open `index.js` and import the `superhero` module:

```
const superhero = require('./superhero.js');

console.log(superhero.getName()); // Output: Batman

superhero.setName('Superman');
console.log(superhero.getName()); // Output: Superman

const newSuperhero = require('./superhero.js');
console.log(newSuperhero.getName()); // Output: Superman
```

In this code, we first import the `superhero` module and store the returned value in a constant named `superhero`. We then call `getName` to print the initial name, which is 'Batman'. We change the name to 'Superman' using `setName` and print the name again.

Next, we import the `superhero` module again to create another instance called `newSuperhero`. However, when we log `newSuperhero.getName`, we still see 'Superman' instead of 'Batman'. Why?

This is where module caching comes in. When we use `require` to import a module, Node.js loads and caches it for future use. This means that the next time we require the same module, Node.js won't load it from scratch. Instead, it uses the cached version.

In our case, when we import `superhero.js` the first time, Node.js caches it. Since we're exporting an instance of the `Superhero` class, the cached version is a reference to that very instance. Therefore, when we import the module again, we're essentially working with the same `Superhero` object that was created initially, and whose name was modified to 'Superman'. This is why both `superhero.getName` and `newSuperhero.getName` return 'Superman'.

Hopefully, this clears up the concept of module caching. But what if we need to create separate instances of the `Superhero` class?

Let's update our code. Instead of exporting an instance of the class, we'll export the class itself:

```
module.exports = Superhero; // Export the class instead
of an instance
```

Now, we'll modify our `index.js`:

```
const Superhero = require('./superhero.js'); // Import
the class

const batman = new Superhero('Batman');
console.log(batman.getName()); // Output: Batman

batman.setName('Bruce Wayne');
console.log(batman.getName()); // Output: Bruce Wayne

const superman = new Superhero('Superman');
console.log(superman.getName()); // Output: Superman
```

Here, we import the `Superhero` class. We create two instances, `batman` and `superman`, with their respective names. Now, we can call `getName` and `setName` on each instance separately, resulting in distinct behaviors for each superhero.

When you run this code, you'll see the output as expected: `Batman`, `Bruce Wayne`, and `Superman`.

Remember, understanding how modules are imported and exported is crucial to avoid unexpected bugs. Keep this in mind as you build your Node.js applications.

Import Export Patterns

In this lesson, we're going to explore some common patterns for importing and exporting modules in Node.js. These patterns are useful for organizing your code and making it easier to reuse functions and variables across different parts of your project.

We'll start by creating a new file called `math.js`. Inside this file, we'll define a simple function that adds two numbers:

```
// math.js
function add(a, b) {
    return a + b;
}

// We can export the add function using module.exports
module.exports = add;
```

Now, in a separate file called `index.js`, we'll import the `add` function and use it:

```
// index.js
const add = require('./math'); // Import the add function
from math.js

console.log(add(2, 3));   // Output: 5
```

To run this code, open your terminal and navigate to the directory where these files are located. Then type `node index.js` and press Enter. You should see the output 5 in your terminal.

This is the simplest pattern for exporting and importing modules. We can also directly assign the function to `module.exports` like this:

```
// math.js
module.exports = function add(a, b) {
    return a + b;
}
```

This pattern is equivalent to the first one and produces the same result.

Let's explore exporting multiple functions. In `math.js`, we'll add another function called `subtract`:

```
// math.js
function add(a, b) {
  return a + b;
}

function subtract(a, b) {
  return a - b;
}

// Export both functions using an object
module.exports = {
  add,
  subtract,
};
```

Now, in `index.js`, we can import and use both functions:

```
// index.js
const math = require('./math');

console.log(math.add(2, 3));       // Output: 5
console.log(math.subtract(2, 3));  // Output: -1
```

Run `node index.js` again, and you'll see both 5 and -1 printed in the terminal.

We can also use object destructuring to import specific functions from the exported object:

```
// index.js
const { add, subtract } = require('./math');

console.log(add(2, 3));       // Output: 5
console.log(subtract(2, 3));  // Output: -1
```

Another pattern is to directly assign functions to properties of `module.exports`:

```
// math.js
module.exports.add = function(a, b) {
  return a + b;
};

module.exports.subtract = function(a, b) {
  return a - b;
};
```

This pattern is similar to the previous one where we created an object, but it directly assigns the functions to properties of `module.exports`.

Finally, we can use the `exports` object, which is a reference to `module.exports`, to export our functions:

```
// math.js
exports.add = function(a, b) {
  return a + b;
};

exports.subtract = function(a, b) {
  return a - b;
};
```

This pattern works because `exports` is a reference to `module.exports`, but it is discouraged because it can lead to unexpected behavior in larger projects. Stick to using `module.exports` to avoid any potential problems.

Exercise: Create a new file called `calculator.js` and define functions for multiplication and division. Export these functions using the `module.exports` object. Then, create a file called `useCalculator.js` and import the multiplication and division functions from `calculator.js`. Use them to calculate 10 * 5 and 10 / 2 and print the results to the console.

Solution:

calculator.js

```
function multiply(a, b) {
  return a * b;
}

function divide(a, b) {
  return a / b;
}

module.exports = {
  multiply,
  divide,
};
```

useCalculator.js

```
const { multiply, divide } = require('./calculator');
```

```
console.log(multiply(10, 5)); // Output: 50
console.log(divide(10, 2)); // Output: 5
```

Remember to run `node useCalculator.js` in your terminal to see the results.

We've explored various ways to import and export modules in Node.js. While these patterns may seem different, they all serve the same purpose: organizing your code and making it reusable. Keep experimenting with these patterns and find the ones that best suit your needs and coding style.

Module.Exports vs Exports

In the last lesson, we discussed different ways to import and export modules. We learned about the `exports` keyword, which can be used as a shortcut for `module.exports`. But, I mentioned that it's generally better to use `module.exports` instead of `exports`. Let's understand why!

Imagine you have two objects: `obj1` and `obj2`. If you assign `obj1` to `obj2`, they actually point to the same memory location. Any changes made to `obj2` will also affect `obj1`.

```
// object_reference.js
const obj1 = { name: 'Bruce Wayne' };
const obj2 = obj1;
obj2.name = 'Clark Kent';

console.log(obj1);
```

Output:
```
{ name: 'Clark Kent' }
```

This happens because JavaScript uses references for objects. Changing `obj2` modifies the original `obj1` data.

However, if you later assign a completely **new** object to `obj2`, the reference is broken. Changes to `obj2` won't affect `obj1` anymore.

```
// object_reference.js
const obj1 = { name: 'Bruce Wayne' };
let obj2 = obj1;
obj2 = { name: 'Clark Kent' };
```

```
console.log(obj1);
```
Output:
```
{ name: 'Bruce Wayne' }
```

Now, let's relate this to `module.exports` and `exports`. In Node.js, `module.exports` is like `obj1` and `exports` is like `obj2`. Both initially point to the same empty object.

```
// math.js
exports.add = (a, b) => a + b;
exports.subtract = (a, b) => a - b;
```
Output:
```
// index.js
const math = require('./math.js');
console.log(math.add(5, 3)); // 8
console.log(math.subtract(5, 3)); // 2
```

This works because we are adding properties (`add` and `subtract`) to the same object (`exports` and `module.exports`) which are referenced by both.

However, if we directly assign a **new** object to `exports`, the reference breaks.

```
// math.js
exports = {
  add: (a, b) => a + b,
  subtract: (a, b) => a - b,
};
```
Output:
```
// index.js
const math = require('./math.js');
console.log(math.add(5, 3)); // Error: Cannot read
properties of undefined (reading 'add')
```

This causes an error because `module.exports` becomes empty, and `math` in `index.js` doesn't have the `add` and `subtract` functions, and it looks inside module.exports not exports.

The key takeaway is:

- **Modifying the** `exports` **object using** `.add`, `.subtract`, **etc. works fine because it modifies both** `exports` **and** `module.exports`.
- **Directly assigning a new object to** `exports` **breaks the reference**

and `module.exports` **becomes empty.**

Since directly assigning to `exports` is prone to errors, it's considered best practice to use `module.exports` for exporting objects from your modules. Although `exports` is shorter, the potential confusion and errors are not worth it!

Now you have a clear understanding of `module.exports`, `exports`, and why it's better to use `module.exports` consistently.

Exercise:

Create a module called `calculator.js` that exports functions for `add`, `subtract`, `multiply`, and `divide`. Use `module.exports` to export these functions.

Create another file `main.js` that imports the `calculator` module and uses its functions to perform some calculations.

Solution:

calculator.js:

```js
module.exports = {
  add: (a, b) => a + b,
  subtract: (a, b) => a - b,
  multiply: (a, b) => a * b,
  divide: (a, b) => {
    if (b === 0) {
      return 'Cannot divide by zero';
    } else {
      return a / b;
    }
  },
};
```

main.js:

```js
const calculator = require('./calculator.js');

console.log(calculator.add(5, 3));
console.log(calculator.subtract(5, 3));
console.log(calculator.multiply(5, 3));
console.log(calculator.divide(5, 3));
console.log(calculator.divide(5, 0));
```

ES Modules

So far we've been using the CommonJS module format in Node.js. This works perfectly fine, but there's a newer, more standard way to handle modules, and that's **ES Modules** (ESM).

You might be wondering, why do we need another way to import and export modules? Well, when Node.js was first created, JavaScript didn't have a built-in module system. So Node.js used CommonJS as the go-to solution. But, with ES2015 (also known as ES6), JavaScript finally got its own standardized module system - **ES Modules**!

It took a while for browsers and Node.js to fully adopt this new standard. But, with Node.js version 14, ES Modules became stable and widely supported.

To understand how ES Modules work, let's use our trusty "math" module example. Let's create a similar example, but this time, we'll use ES Modules.

Create your Files:

- `main.mjs`: This file will be our main entry point.
- `math-esm.mjs`: This file will contain our math functions.

`math-esm.mjs`:

```
// math-esm.mjs
export default function add(a, b) {
  return a + b;
}
```

`main.mjs`:

```
// main.mjs
import add from './math-esm.mjs';

console.log(add(5, 5)); // Output: 10
```

Notice that in `math-esm.mjs`, we use `export default` to export our `add` function. In `main.mjs`, we use `import` to bring in the `add` function. It's like opening a door to a library and grabbing the specific book we need!

You should see the output `10` in your terminal.

Another Pattern:

```
// math-esm.mjs
export default (a, b) => {
  return a + b;
};
```

We can also include the `export default` directly in line with our arrow function. This makes our code even more concise. Run `node main.mjs` again, and you'll see the same output.

Exporting Multiple Functions:

In ESM, we also have something called named exports. This is similar to the previous example, but we use the `export` keyword directly on the functions themselves.

```
// math-esm.mjs
export const add = (a, b) => a + b;
export const subtract = (a, b) => a - b;
```

Now, we're exporting both the `add` and `subtract` functions. In our `main.mjs` file, we can import both of them using an object:

```
// main.mjs
import * as math from './math-esm.mjs';

console.log(math.add(5, 5));      // Output: 10
console.log(math.subtract(5, 5)); // Output: 0
```

We can also use **destructuring**, which allows us to directly extract the functions we need from the object:

```
// main.mjs
import { add, subtract } from './math-esm.mjs';

console.log(add(5, 5));      // Output: 10
console.log(subtract(5, 5)); // Output: 0
```

Exercise:

Create a new file called `calculator-esm.mjs`. This file should contain functions for basic calculator operations: `add`, `subtract`, `multiply`, and `divide`. Export these functions using named exports. Then, create a `main.mjs` file that imports these functions and uses them to perform some calculations.

Solution:

calculator-esm.mjs:

```
export const add = (a, b) => a + b;
export const subtract = (a, b) => a - b;
export const multiply = (a, b) => a * b;
export const divide = (a, b) => a / b;
```

main.mjs:

```
import { add, subtract, multiply, divide } from
'./calculator-esm.mjs';

console.log(add(5, 5)); // Output: 10
console.log(subtract(5, 5)); // Output: 0
console.log(multiply(5, 5)); // Output: 25
console.log(divide(10, 2)); // Output: 5
```

Give it a try and see how ES Modules can make your Node.js projects more organized and efficient!

Importing JSON

We'll learn how to import JSON data into our Node.js projects. JSON, or JavaScript Object Notation, is a super common data format used with web servers to exchange information. So, how does importing JSON files work in Node.js?

Let's start by creating a new file called data.json in our project folder. You can think of a JSON file like a JavaScript object, but with the keys wrapped in quotes. Inside this data.json file, let's add some sample data.

```
{
  "name": "Bruce Wayne",
  "address": {
    "street": "Main Manor",
    "city": "Gotham"
  }
}
```

Now, open up your index.js file and we'll load the data from this JSON file.

```
const data = require('./data.json');
console.log(data);
```

The require function is our friend here. We use it to import the data.json file and store it in the data variable. When we run node index.js in the terminal, you'll see that the JSON data is printed as a JavaScript object.

That's the default behavior in Node.js – it automatically parses JSON files into JavaScript objects for us! Now, we can access the data like any regular JavaScript object. For example, to display Bruce Wayne's name, we can use data.name.

```
const data = require('./data.json');
console.log(data.name);
```

One thing to remember is that you can skip the .json extension when importing a JSON file. You can simply use require('./data'). But, here's a heads-up! Node.js will first look for a file called data.js before looking for data.json. So, if a data.js file exists, Node.js will import that instead of the JSON file, which could lead to some unexpected behavior.

It's best practice to always use the .json extension when importing JSON files.

Built-in Modules

They're like pre-made tools that come with your Node.js toolbox. Think of them as pre-installed apps on your phone, ready to use whenever you need them.

These built-in modules are like magic helpers, they simplify your coding tasks and give you access to features you might otherwise have to build from scratch. In this lesson, we're going to focus on five super useful built-in modules: path, os, events, fs, stream, and http.

The path module is the easiest to grasp. Imagine you have a bunch of files on your computer, and you want to know their location, name, or how to find a specific file. The path module helps you navigate your file system just like a map! Let's see an example:

```
const path = require('path');

const filePath = path.join(__dirname, 'myFile.txt');

console.log(filePath); // Output:
/path/to/your/project/myFile.txt
```

Here, we used `require('path')` to import the `path` module. The `__dirname` variable gives us the current directory where our script is running. The `path.join()` function then helps us combine the current directory with the name of our file (`myFile.txt`) to get the full path to the file.

The remaining four modules – `os`, `events`, `fs`, and `stream` – are a bit more complex, but don't worry, we'll break them down step by step.

Path Module

We're diving into our first built-in module: the *path* module. Think of it as a handy guide for all things related to files and directories. We'll learn how to use it to manipulate file paths and make working with files and folders much easier.

We'll be working in `index.js`, to use a built-in module, we first need to bring it into our project. We do this by using the `require` function. This function acts like a magic portal, allowing us to pull in the module we need.

```
const path = require('path');
```

Here, we're assigning the path module to a variable called `path`. It's important to use `'path'` inside the `require` function because that's the name of the module we want. Notice that we don't need to add a dot slash (`.`) at the beginning.

Once we've imported the module, we can start using its special powers – its properties and methods. The `path` module has a whole bunch of these tools, but Now, we'll be focusing on seven that are super useful in everyday coding.

But before we get into those methods, let's quickly review two special variables that are automatically available in every module: `__filename` and `__dirname`.

```
console.log(__filename);
console.log(__dirname);
```

If we run this code using `node index.js`, you'll see something like this:

```
/Users/yourname/node.js/index.js
```

```
/Users/yourname/node.js
```

__filename gives us the full path to our index.js file, while __dirname tells us the full path to the folder where index.js lives, in this case, the project folder.

Now, let's explore those seven awesome methods of the path module!

1. basename(path):

This method helps us extract the last part of a path. Let's see it in action:

```
console.log(path.basename(__filename));
console.log(path.basename(__dirname));
```

Running this code will output:

```
index.js
node.js
```

As you can see, basename extracts "index.js" from __filenameand "node.js" from __dirname. It's like getting the name of the file or folder without all the extra directory information.

2. extname(path):

This method is all about file extensions. It tells us what kind of file it is by extracting the part after the dot (.) in a path.

```
console.log(path.extname(__filename));
console.log(path.extname(__dirname));
```

If we run this code, we'll get:

```
.js
```

Since __dirname doesn't have a dot, extname returns an empty string.

3. parse(path):

This method is a bit more powerful. It breaks down a path into its individual components, giving us a neat object with lots of useful information.

```
console.log(path.parse(__filename));
```

This will output something like:

```
{
  root: '/',
```

```
    dir: '/Users/yourname/node.js',
    base: 'index.js',
    ext: '.js',
    name: 'index'
}
```

We get a dictionary with keys like `root`, `dir`, `base`, `ext`, and `name`, each providing a specific part of the path. We can access these individual properties using dot notation, just like any regular object.

4. `format(pathObject)`:

`format` works in reverse. It takes an object like the one we got from `parse` and stitches it back together into a proper path string.

```
console.log(path.format(path.parse(__filename)));
```

This will simply output the original path:

```
/Users/yourname/node.js/index.js
```

5. `isAbsolute(path)`:

This method helps us determine if a path is absolute or relative. An absolute path starts with a slash (/) and represents a location from the root of the file system. A relative path is a path relative to the current working directory.

```
console.log(path.isAbsolute(__filename));
console.log(path.isAbsolute('./data.json'));
```

Running this code, we'll get:

```
true
false
```

`__filename` is an absolute path, but `'./data.json'` is relative to the current directory.

6. `join(path1, path2, ...)`:

This method is all about joining paths together. It takes multiple path segments as arguments and combines them using the appropriate separator for your operating system (slash / for Mac and Linux, backslash \ for Windows).

```
console.log(path.join('folder1', 'folder2',
'index.html'));
console.log(path.join('/', 'folder1', 'folder2',
'index.html'));
```

```
console.log(path.join('folder1', '//folder2',
'index.html'));
console.log(path.join('folder1', '..', 'index.html'));
console.log(path.join(__dirname, 'data.json'));
```

Output:

```
folder1/folder2/index.html
/folder1/folder2/index.html
folder1/folder2/index.html
folder1/index.html
/Users/yourname/node.js/data.json
```

As you can see, `join` not only combines paths but also takes care of removing unnecessary slashes and handles relative path navigation (`..` jumps one folder up).

7. `resolve(path1, path2, ...)`:

This method takes a sequence of paths and converts them into a single, absolute path. It's like a path detective, figuring out the full path by taking into account relative paths and resolving any ambiguity.

```
console.log(path.resolve('folder1', 'folder2',
'index.html'));
console.log(path.resolve('/', 'folder1', 'folder2',
'index.html'));
console.log(path.resolve('folder1', '/folder2',
'index.html'));
console.log(path.resolve('folder1', '..', 'index.html'));
console.log(path.resolve(__dirname, 'data.json'));
```

Output:

```
/Users/yourname/node.js/folder1/folder2/index.html
/folder1/folder2/index.html
/folder2/index.html
/Users/yourname/node.js/index.html
/Users/yourname/node.js/data.json
```

It figures out the complete path from the current directory, taking into account the root path (`/`) and relative navigation (`..`).

You might have noticed that when importing the `path` module, the `node:` prefix is optional. This means you can simply write `require('path')` instead of `require('node:path')`.

However, using the `node:` prefix is highly recommended. It makes it crystal clear that we're using a built-in module and helps avoid any potential conflicts in the future.

Let's recap what we've learned: the `path` module provides a set of powerful tools for working with file and directory paths. We explored several useful methods like `basename`, `extname`, `parse`, `format`, `isAbsolute`, `join`, and `resolve`. Now, you can confidently navigate files and directories like a pro.

Callback Pattern

We need to understand the **callback pattern**. This is a very common style of programming in Node.js and it's essential to grasp its concept.

Let's start with a key idea in JavaScript: **functions are first-class objects**. What does this mean? It means we can treat functions just like any other JavaScript object. We can pass them as arguments to other functions, and we can even return them as values from other functions.

Let's see an example to make this clearer.

Code Example:

```
// Define a function that greets someone
function greet(name) {
  console.log(`Hello ${name}`);
}

// Define a function that calls another function
function greetDavid(greetFN) {
  const name = "David";
  greetFN(name); // Call the passed function
}

// Call the function that accepts another function
greetDavid(greet);

// Output in the terminal: Hello David
```

In this code, `greetDavid` is a function that takes another function, `greet`, as an argument. When `greetDavid` is called, it passes the `greet` function as an argument to `greetFN` and calls it. This is how functions can be treated as objects in JavaScript.

Callback Functions:

Any function passed as an argument to another function is called a **callback function**. The function that accepts a function as an argument or returns a function is called a **higher-order function**. In our example, greet is the callback function and greetDavid is the higher-order function.

You might be thinking: "Why do we need callback functions?" Well, callbacks are essential in Node.js for handling **asynchronous operations**.

Synchronous vs. Asynchronous Callbacks:

We can classify callbacks into two categories:

- **Synchronous Callbacks:** These callbacks execute immediately when the higher-order function calls them. For example, the callback functions we pass to methods like sort, map, or filter are synchronous. The callback defines a logic that the higher-order function needs to apply.

- **Asynchronous Callbacks:** These callbacks are often used to continue or resume code execution after an asynchronous operation has completed.

In the asynchronous programming, callbacks are used to delay the execution of a function until a particular time or event has occurred.

The callback pattern is incredibly popular in Node.js. It helps handle asynchronous operations like:
- Reading data from a file
- Fetching data from a database
- Handling network requests

These operations take time to complete, and we don't want our Node.js program to wait and become unresponsive. Callbacks allow us to handle these asynchronous actions gracefully, letting the program continue with other tasks while the asynchronous operation runs in the background.

Events Module

We'll dive into the second built-in Node.js module: the Events Module.

This module allows us to work with **events**, which are actions or occurrences that happen within our application. With the Events Module, we can respond to these events in a non-blocking way. Think of it as creating a system where different parts of your program can "talk" to each other, reacting to specific happenings.

Let's imagine a real-life scenario: you're hungry and go to Domino's for pizza. At the counter, you place your order. The line cook sees your order on their screen and starts baking your pizza.

This scenario perfectly illustrates how events work. The event is "**placing an order**". The response to that event is "**baking a pizza**".

Now, let's recreate this scenario using Node.js's built-in Events Module!

First, we need to create a file called `index.js`. This file will act as our main module. Open `index.js` and let's get coding!

```js
const EventEmitter = require('events'); // Import the Events Module
const emitter = new EventEmitter(); // Create a new EventEmitter object


// Listen for the 'orderPizza' event
emitter.on('orderPizza', (size, topping) => {
  console.log(`Order received. Baking a ${size} pizza with ${topping}.`);
});

// Emit the 'orderPizza' event
emitter.emit('orderPizza', 'large', 'mushroom'); // Pass pizza size and topping as arguments
```

We start by importing the `events` module using `require('events')`. Notice we're calling our constant `EventEmitter` (with a capital 'E') because the `events` module actually returns a class named `EventEmitter`. This class lets us create objects that can emit and handle events.

Next, we create a new `EventEmitter` object called `emitter`.

Then, we use `emitter.emit('orderPizza', 'large', 'mushroom')` to emit the `orderPizza` event. We also pass the pizza size (large) and topping (mushroom) as arguments.

The emitter.on('orderPizza', (size, topping) => { ... }) line registers a listener for the orderPizza event. This listener is a callback function that gets executed whenever the orderPizza event is emitted. The listener receives the size and topping arguments that were passed when the event was emitted.

Now, run node index.js and you'll see the message "Order received. Baking a large pizza with mushroom." printed on your console.

We can even have multiple listeners for the same event, adding more actions or reactions to a single event.

```
const EventEmitter = require('events');
const emitter = new EventEmitter();

emitter.on('orderPizza', (size, topping) => {
  console.log(`Order received. Baking a ${size} pizza
with ${topping}.`);
});

emitter.on('orderPizza', (size, topping) => {
  if (size === 'large') {
    console.log('Serving a complementary drink!');
  }
});


emitter.emit('orderPizza', 'large', 'mushroom');
```

Here, we have two listeners for the orderPizza event. The first listener prints a basic message about the order, while the second listener checks if the pizza size is large. If it is, it prints a message about serving a complimentary drink.

Run node index.js and you'll see both messages appear on your console.

Remember, these event listeners execute in a non-blocking way. If you add a log statement before the emitter.emit('orderPizza', ...), you'll see that the statement executes first, followed by the messages from your event listeners. This demonstrates the asynchronous nature of event-driven programming.

The Events Module is a powerful tool in Node.js. It allows us to create more dynamic and responsive applications.

Exercise:

Create a Node.js program that simulates a user logging in. Use the `EventEmitter` class to create an event called `'login'`. When the `'login'` event is emitted, a listener should print a welcome message with the user's name.

Solution:

```
const EventEmitter = require('events');
const emitter = new EventEmitter();


emitter.on('login', (username) => {
  console.log(`Welcome, ${username}!`);
});

emitter.emit('login', 'John Doe');
```

Extending EventEmitter

In the previous lesson, we explored the power of the events module. We learned how to use the Event Emitter class to emit and listen to events. In this lesson, we're going to dive deeper and see how we can create our own custom modules that inherit from the Event Emitter class. This is a powerful technique that allows our modules to participate in the event-driven architecture of Node.js.

Let's imagine we're building a pizza shop application. We want to create a `PizzaShop` class that handles orders and interacts with other parts of our application through events. First, create a new file named `pizzashop.js` and paste in the following code:

```
class PizzaShop {
  constructor() {
    this.orderNumber = 0;
  }

  placeOrder() {
    this.orderNumber++;
    console.log(`Order number: ${this.orderNumber}`);
  }
```

```
displayOrderNumber() {
    console.log(`Current order number: $
{this.orderNumber}`);
  }
}

module.exports = PizzaShop;
```

Here, we define the `PizzaShop` class with a constructor to initialize the `orderNumber` to zero and methods like `placeOrder` to increment the order number and `displayOrderNumber` to show the current order number. We export the class using `module.exports` so we can use it in other parts of our application.

Now, let's open our `index.js` file and import the `PizzaShop` class.

```
// index.js

const PizzaShop = require('./pizzashop');

const pizzaShop = new PizzaShop();
pizzaShop.placeOrder();
pizzaShop.displayOrderNumber();
```

If we run `node index.js` in our terminal, we should see the following output:

```
Order number: 1
Current order number: 1
```

This simple code shows that our `PizzaShop` class is working perfectly, but we want to integrate it with the event-driven architecture of Node.js. We can achieve this by using inheritance. In JavaScript, we can extend one class to inherit the functionality of another class. This is exactly what we want to do with our `PizzaShop` class – we want it to inherit from the `EventEmitter` class.

Let's modify our `pizzashop.js` file.

```
const EventEmitter = require('events');

class PizzaShop extends EventEmitter {
  constructor() {
    super();
    this.orderNumber = 0;
  }
```

```
  placeOrder(size, toppings) {
    this.orderNumber++;
    console.log(`Order number: ${this.orderNumber}`);
    this.emit('order', size, toppings); // Emit the order
event
  }

  displayOrderNumber() {
    console.log(`Current order number: $
{this.orderNumber}`);
  }
}

module.exports = PizzaShop;
```

Now, our `PizzaShop` class can emit events! Let's move on to `index.js` and add listeners to handle those events.

```
// index.js

const PizzaShop = require('./pizzashop');
const DrinkMachine = require('./drinkmachine'); // We'll
create this later

const pizzaShop = new PizzaShop();

pizzaShop.on('order', (size, toppings) => {
  console.log(`Order received! Making a ${size} pizza
with ${toppings}.`);
  DrinkMachine.serveDrink(size); // Call the serveDrink
method
});

pizzaShop.placeOrder('large', 'mushrooms');
pizzaShop.displayOrderNumber();
```

Here we add an event listener for the `order` event using `pizzaShop.on('order', ...)` and handle the received `size` and `toppings`.

Now, let's create a new file called `drinkmachine.js` to handle serving complimentary drinks based on the order size.

```
// drinkmachine.js
class DrinkMachine {
  serveDrink(size) {
    if (size === 'large') {
      console.log('Serving complimentary drink!');
```

```
    }
  }
}
```

```
module.exports = DrinkMachine;
```

We export the `DrinkMachine` class so we can use it in `index.js`.

Finally, we run `node index.js` and get the following output:

```
Order number: 1
Order received! Making a large pizza with mushrooms.
Serving complimentary drink!
Current order number: 1
```

Our code is now working! Our `PizzaShop` class is extending the `EventEmitter` class and emitting events. Our `index.js` file is listening for those events, handling them, and interacting with other modules like `DrinkMachine` through events.

This shows how using events can help us build loosely coupled, flexible, and modular applications. Remember, most of the built-in Node.js modules like `fs`, `streams`, and `http` are also built upon the `EventEmitter` class. You can use this knowledge to work with these modules effectively in your Node.js projects.

Exercise

Create a new module named `delivery.js` that handles delivery notifications. In this module, create a `DeliveryService` class which extends `EventEmitter`. Make the `DeliveryService` class emit a `delivered` event when a delivery is completed. Modify `index.js` to listen for the `delivered` event and log a message confirming the delivery.

Solution

```
// delivery.js
const EventEmitter = require('events');

class DeliveryService extends EventEmitter {
  deliverOrder() {
    // Simulate delivery process
    setTimeout(() => {
      this.emit('delivered');
      console.log('Delivery completed!');
```

```
    }, 2000);
  }
}

module.exports = DeliveryService;
// index.js
const PizzaShop = require('./pizzashop');
const DrinkMachine = require('./drinkmachine');
const DeliveryService = require('./delivery');

const pizzaShop = new PizzaShop();
const deliveryService = new DeliveryService();

pizzaShop.on('order', (size, toppings) => {
  console.log(`Order received! Making a ${size} pizza
with ${toppings}.`);
  DrinkMachine.serveDrink(size);
  deliveryService.deliverOrder(); // Initiate delivery
});

deliveryService.on('delivered', () => {
  console.log('Delivery confirmed!');
});

pizzaShop.placeOrder('large', 'mushrooms');
pizzaShop.displayOrderNumber();
```

This example demonstrates how we can chain events together to create complex workflows.

By now, you have a strong understanding of how to create custom modules that extend the Event Emitter class. This technique allows your modules to integrate smoothly into Node.js's event-driven architecture, creating flexible and reusable code.

Character Sets and Encoding

We've learned about the path and events modules. Now, before we move on to the remaining built-in modules, we need to understand character sets, encoding, streams, and buffers. We'll start with character sets and encoding.

Binary Data

Think of computers as giant storage units filled with tiny switches, each switch representing a **bit**. These switches can be either "on" (1) or "off" (0). To store data, computers use **binary**, a system of ones and zeros. For example, the number 4 in binary is `100`. To understand how this works, think about a light switch. If it's "on", it's 1, and if it's "off", it's 0. We can use this to represent numbers, with each place value representing a power of 2. So, `100` in binary is $(2^2 * 1) + (2^1 * 0) + (2^0 * 0)$, which equals 4.

Character Representation

But computers don't just store numbers. They also need to store text, like the letter "V". To represent characters in binary, computers first convert the character to a number, and then convert that number to binary. For example, the character "V" has a character code of 86. This means the computer uses the number 86 to represent the character "V" in the computer's memory. You can see this in your browser's dev tools console by typing `"V".charCodeAt()`.

Character Sets

So, how does the computer know that 86 represents the letter "V"? This is where **character sets** come in. They're basically a table that maps characters to their corresponding numbers. Two popular character sets are **ASCII** and **Unicode**. Unicode is what you saw in the browser example, where "V" is assigned the code point 86. You can check out websites like unicodeable.com to see how different characters are represented in Unicode.

Character Encoding

Now, we know that characters are represented by numbers, but how does the computer store those numbers in binary format? That's where **character encoding** comes in. It tells the computer how many bits to use to represent a number in binary. One common encoding system is **UTF-8**. UTF-8 encodes characters in **bytes**, which are groups of 8 bits. For example, the number 4 in binary is `100`. With UTF-8 encoding, the computer adds five zeros to the left to make it a byte, so it becomes `00000100`. Similarly, "D" with a code point of 68 is represented as `00100100` in binary.

This is how computers store characters or strings in binary format.

Remember, similar guidelines exist for storing images and lessons as well, but we'll dive into that in later lessons.

Now, you know what binary data, character sets, and character encoding are. This knowledge is crucial for understanding how computers handle text data.

Asynchronous JavaScript

It might sound a bit complicated, but trust me, it's not as scary as it seems. In fact, it's incredibly powerful and plays a crucial role in making our Node.js applications efficient and responsive.

Think about it like this: JavaScript, in its most basic form, is like a single person trying to do many things at once. Let's say they have a long list of tasks. They can only focus on one task at a time. If one task takes a long time, like waiting for information from a database, everything else gets stuck until that task is finished. This is like a single-threaded, blocking, synchronous language! It works, but it can be really slow and inefficient, especially when we need to do things like retrieve data from the internet or read from a file system. That's where asynchronous JavaScript comes in!

Imagine our single person having a helper. This helper can take over some tasks while our main person continues with other things. If our main person needs to wait for something like database information, they can ask the helper to get it while they continue with other tasks. When the helper is done, it can alert our main person, and they can resume their work without having to wait! That's how asynchronous JavaScript works!

Now, how does this work in the real world? JavaScript on its own can't directly handle these asynchronous tasks. We need some extra help! In the browser, it's the browser itself, and in the backend, it's Node.js. These platforms provide special functions and tools that let us register actions to be executed asynchronously when certain events happen, like:

- **Time passing:** We can schedule tasks to run after a certain period.
- **User interaction:** We can trigger actions when the user clicks a button or moves their mouse.

- **Data arrival:** We can handle data coming in from a file or over the internet.

This means that while our main JavaScript thread is busy doing other things, these helper functions can work in the background and notify our main program when they're finished. This is how we achieve the non-blocking, asynchronous behavior that's crucial for modern applications.

It's what makes Node.js so fast and efficient. So, while JavaScript itself is synchronous, the magic of Node.js and browsers enables us to write asynchronous code, making our applications more powerful and responsive!

Streams and Buffers

In the last lesson, we explored the world of binary data – the zeros and ones that computers understand. We also learned about character sets, which are lists of characters represented by numbers, and how character encoding translates these numbers into binary data.

Now, let's dive into **streams** and **buffers**.

Imagine you're watching a lesson on YouTube. You don't have to wait for the entire lesson to download before you can start watching, right? Instead, the lesson data arrives in small chunks, and you watch it in those chunks as the rest of the data keeps coming. This is the power of streams!

In simple terms, a **stream** is like a continuous flow of data. It can be data coming from the internet, a file, or even a microphone. Node.js processes these data streams in chunks, without waiting for the whole thing to be available. This approach saves time and memory, making your applications more efficient.

But how does Node.js handle these chunks of data? That's where **buffers** come in.

Think of a **buffer** like the waiting area at an amusement park. Imagine a roller coaster that can fit 30 people at a time. People arrive at the ride at different paces. Sometimes a big group shows up, sometimes just one person.

The buffer is where these people wait. You can't control how many people arrive at once, but you can decide when to send them on the ride. If the roller coaster is full or there aren't enough people to start, you'll need a buffer to hold the waiting passengers.

Similarly, Node.js can't control the speed at which data arrives in a stream. It can only decide when to process it. If there's already data being processed or not enough data to process, Node.js puts the incoming data into a buffer. This is a temporary holding area for data chunks until they are ready for processing.

A good example of a buffer in action is when you're streaming a lesson online. If your internet connection is fast, the stream will fill the buffer quickly and the lesson will play smoothly. But if your connection is slow, the buffer might empty before the next chunk arrives, resulting in a "loading spinner" while it waits for more data.

Now, let's connect the dots! How do buffers relate to the binary data, character sets, and encoding we learned about in the previous lesson?

Let's hop back to the editor and write some code!

```
// index.js
const buffer = Buffer.from('David', 'utf-8');

console.log(buffer.toJSON());
console.log(buffer);
console.log(buffer.toString());

buffer.write('code');

console.log(buffer.toString());
```

Output:

```
{
  "type": "Buffer",
  "data": [86, 105, 115, 104, 119, 97, 115]
}
<Buffer 56 69 73 68 77 61 73>
David
coded
```

Let's break down what's happening here:

• We create a buffer using `Buffer.from()`. It takes a string (`'David'`) and an optional character encoding (we're using `'utf-8'`).

- `buffer.toJSON()` shows us the buffer's contents as an object. The key piece is the `data` array, which holds the Unicode character codes for each letter in our string. Notice that 'V' is represented by the number 86, just like we learned about in the last lesson.
- `console.log(buffer)` displays the buffer's raw binary data in hexadecimal format. Each hexadecimal number corresponds to an 8-bit binary representation of a character.
- `buffer.toString()` converts the buffer back to a string.
- `buffer.write()` modifies the buffer's contents. In this case, we're writing the string 'code'. Because buffers have limited memory, the new data overwrites part of the original data, changing the string to 'coded'.

This exercise illustrates how buffers hold raw binary data and can be manipulated to represent various data types.

Remember: While Node.js uses buffers extensively behind the scenes, you don't always have to work with them directly. But understanding how they work gives you a deeper grasp of how Node.js processes data.

fs

Think of it as your toolset to manage files on your computer. We'll break it down so it's super easy to understand, even if you're a complete beginner!

Let's start by creating a new file named `index.js`. This is where we'll write our Node.js code. Now, to use the `fs` module, we need to import it. Just like getting a tool from your toolbox, we "import" it into our project. We do this using the `require` function at the top of our `index.js` file:

```
const fs = require('fs');
```

Now, `fs` is like our toolbox, containing all the tools we need to work with files! Let's grab one of those tools: the `readFileSync` method! This tool lets us read the contents of a file.

First, let's create a file named `file.txt`. We'll put the text "Hello David Mark" inside. Now, back in `index.js`, we'll use our `readFileSync` tool like this:

```
const fs = require('fs');

const fileContents = fs.readFileSync('./file.txt');
console.log(fileContents);
```

If you run `node index.js` now, you'll see some weird characters on the console. That's because `readFileSync` gives you the raw data in binary format. Don't worry, we can fix that! Just add a second argument, `'utf-8'`, to the `readFileSync` method:

```
const fs = require('fs');

const fileContents = fs.readFileSync('./file.txt', 'utf-8');
console.log(fileContents);
```

Run `node index.js` again, and you'll see the familiar text "Hello David Mark" printed on the console! This is because `'utf-8'` tells Node.js to decode the data from binary into human-readable text.

Important! The `readFileSync` method is **synchronous**. This means Node.js will wait until the file is completely read before moving on to the next line of code. Think of it as waiting for the file to be downloaded before continuing. This might be okay for small files, but for larger files, it can cause your program to slow down.

Node.js is all about being efficient, and it's designed for asynchronous tasks. So, for reading files, there's also the `readFile` method. This method is **asynchronous**, which means it doesn't wait for the file to be read before continuing. Instead, it uses a callback function that gets executed when the file is done reading.

Let's modify our `index.js` to use `readFile`:

```
const fs = require('fs');

fs.readFile('./file.txt', 'utf-8', (error, data) => {
  if (error) {
    console.error('Error reading file:', error);
  } else {
    console.log('File contents:', data);
  }
});

console.log('First!');
console.log('Second!');
```

Run `node index.js`. You'll see the "First!" and "Second!" messages printed right away, and then, when the file has been read, you'll see the "File contents" message along with the contents of `file.txt`.

This is the power of asynchronous programming! Node.js doesn't stop and wait for the file to be read. It continues to execute other code, and then, when the file is ready, it runs the callback function. This makes your program much more efficient, especially when you're dealing with many files or users.

The `fs` module also has methods for writing to files! Let's try writing the text "Hello World" to a new file called `greet.txt`. We'll use the `writeFile` method, which also comes in both synchronous and asynchronous versions.

Let's start with the synchronous version, `writeFileSync`:

```
const fs = require('fs');

fs.writeFileSync('./greet.txt', 'Hello World');
```

Now run `node index.js`. You'll see a new file, `greet.txt`, has been created with the text "Hello World" inside! Pretty simple, right?

For asynchronous writing, we'll use `writeFile`:

```
const fs = require('fs');

fs.writeFile('./greet.txt', 'Hello David', (error) => {
  if (error) {
    console.error('Error writing file:', error);
  } else {
    console.log('File written!');
  }
});
```

Again, this uses a callback function that gets executed when the file has been written. If there's an error, the `error` parameter will contain the error object. Otherwise, the `File written!` message will be printed.

Important: By default, `writeFile` overwrites the file if it already exists. To append data to an existing file, you can use the `flag` option:

```
const fs = require('fs');

fs.writeFile('./greet.txt', ' Hello David', { flag:
'a' }, (error) => {
```

```
  if (error) {
    console.error('Error writing file:', error);
  } else {
    console.log('File written!');
  }
});
```

This will add the text `Hello David` (with a space in front) to the end of `greet.txt`.

That's it for the basics of the `fs` module! We've covered reading and writing files both synchronously and asynchronously. This is a powerful set of tools that will help you build awesome file-handling features in your Node.js applications.

Exercise:

Try creating a file called `data.txt` with some text inside. Then, write a Node.js program that reads the contents of this file, counts the number of words, and writes the word count to a new file called `word_count.txt`.

Solution:

```
const fs = require('fs');

fs.readFile('./data.txt', 'utf-8', (error, data) => {
  if (error) {
    console.error('Error reading file:', error);
  } else {
    const words = data.trim().split(/\s+/);
    const wordCount = words.length;

    fs.writeFile('./word_count.txt', `Word Count: $
{wordCount}`, (error) => {
      if (error) {
        console.error('Error writing file:', error);
      } else {
        console.log('Word count written to file!');
      }
    });
  }
});
```

Keep exploring Node.js and the `fs` module.

fs Promise

In previous lesson, we've dealt with file operations using the `fs` module. We've done this using callbacks. But a newer, more modern way to handle these tasks is with promises. Promises are like little containers for future results. You get a promise, and it will eventually resolve with the information you need, or it might reject if something goes wrong.

First, we need to include the `fs` promise module in our project:

```
const fs = require('fs/promises');
```

Let's say we want to read the contents of a file called `file.txt`. We can use the `readFile` method. This method returns a promise, so we'll use `.then` and `.catch` blocks to handle the result:

```
fs.readFile('file.txt', 'utf-8')
    .then((data) => {
        console.log(data);
    })
    .catch((error) => {
        console.error(error);
    });
```

This code will read the file, and if successful, print the contents to the console. If there's an error, it will print the error message.

How it works:

The `readFile` method takes two arguments: the file name and the encoding type (we use `utf-8` for text files). It returns a promise, which is a way to represent an action that will happen in the future.

- The `.then` block is executed when the promise resolves successfully, giving you access to the data.
- The `.catch` block is executed when the promise rejects, providing you with the error information.

This approach makes our code more organized and readable.

Let's try using `async/await`!

`async/await` is a feature in JavaScript that makes dealing with promises even easier. We can use `async/await` to handle promises in a way that looks very similar to regular function calls.

```
async function readFileAsync() {
    try {
        const data = await fs.readFile('file.txt', 'utf-
8');
        console.log(data);
    } catch (error) {
        console.error(error);
    }
}
```

```
readFileAsync();
```

This is a slightly different approach. We use `async` to tell JavaScript that this function might need to wait for some promises to resolve. Inside the function, we use `await` before our promise call. This will pause the function until the promise resolves. If it resolves successfully, we store the data. If it rejects, we catch the error.

While using the promise-based `fs` module is generally a good choice, if you're working on applications where performance is absolutely critical, you might want to use the traditional callback-based `fs` module, as it can offer some small performance advantages.

fs and Streams

In the last couple of lessons, we learned about the `fs` module for working with the file system. Now, let's dive deeper into the `fs` module and learn about streams in Node.js.

Remember, a stream is like a river of data flowing from one place to another. Think of it like transferring a file from your computer to a friend's computer. Instead of sending the entire file at once, we send it in smaller parts, or "chunks," over time. This saves memory and makes the process more efficient.

Node.js has a built-in `stream` module, which inherits from the `EventEmitter` class. This means we can listen for events that happen during the data flow. However, we rarely use the `stream` module directly. Other modules, like `fs`, use streams internally for their operations.

Let's open up VS Code and see how the `fs` module uses streams to read

and write data. I've created an empty file called `file2.txt`. We'll
transfer the contents from `file.txt` to this file using streams.

```
// index.js
const fs = require('fs');

// Create a readable stream to read data from file.txt
const readableStream = fs.createReadStream('./file.txt',
{ encoding: 'utf8' });

// Create a writable stream to write data to file2.txt
const writableStream =
fs.createWriteStream('./file2.txt');

// Listen for the 'data' event on the readable stream
readableStream.on('data', (chunk) => {
  console.log(chunk); // Log the data chunk to the
console
  writableStream.write(chunk); // Write the data chunk to
file2.txt
});
```

Now, if you save `index.js` and run `node index`, you'll see the entire
content of `file.txt` (which is "Hello David Mark") printed to the
console and also written to `file2.txt`.

You might notice that the entire file content was transferred in a single
chunk. That's because the default buffer size for streams is 64
kilobytes, and our file is much smaller. Let's change this behavior by
adding the `highWaterMark` option to the `createReadStream` method.

```
// index.js
const fs = require('fs');

const readableStream = fs.createReadStream('./file.txt',
{
  encoding: 'utf8',
  highWaterMark: 2 // Read data in chunks of 2 bytes
});

const writableStream =
fs.createWriteStream('./file2.txt');

readableStream.on('data', (chunk) => {
  console.log(chunk);
  writableStream.write(chunk);
});
```

Now, if you run `node index`, you'll see the console output is broken into chunks of two characters. This is because we've reduced the `highWaterMark` to 2 bytes. However, `file2.txt` still contains the full text "Hello David Mark".

This might not seem like a big difference with a small file, but imagine working with large files that are megabytes in size. Using streams can significantly speed up the process and save memory.

The `fs` module is just one example of how streams are used. The `http` module, which we'll explore in the next lesson, heavily relies on streams. HTTP requests are readable streams, and HTTP responses are writable streams.

There are actually four types of streams in Node.js:

- **Readable Streams:** Data can be read from them.
- **Writable Streams:** Data can be written to them.
- **Duplex Streams:** Data can be both read and written to them. For example, sockets.
- **Transform Streams:** Data can be modified or transformed as it's read and written. For example, file compression.

Exercise:

Create a new file called `exercise.txt` with some text content. Then, create a Node.js script that reads the content from `exercise.txt`, converts it to uppercase, and writes it to a new file called `uppercase.txt`. Use streams for this task.

Solution:

```
// exercise.js
const fs = require('fs');

const readableStream = fs.createReadStream('./file.txt',
{ encoding: 'utf8' });
const writableStream =
fs.createWriteStream('./uppercase.txt');

readableStream.on('data', (chunk) => {
  writableStream.write(chunk.toUpperCase());
});
```

Pipes

In the previous lesson, we learned about streams, specifically how to read and write file content using `createReadStream` and `createWriteStream`. We saw how these streams are helpful, but Node.js offers an even more efficient and user-friendly way to do the same thing – using **pipes**.

Think of a pipe like a physical one connecting a water tank to a kitchen sink. The tank feeds water into the pipe, and that water gets released through the sink tap. From the pipe's perspective, it reads water from the tank and writes it to the sink.

Node.js pipes work the same way. They connect a readable stream to a writable stream. We use the `pipe` method on a readable stream to establish this connection.

Let's see this in action. Remember our `index.js` file from the previous lesson? We used `data` events to read and write data from a file. With pipes, we can do this with just one line of code.

```
const fs = require('fs');

const readableStream = fs.createReadStream('./file.txt');
const writableStream =
fs.createWriteStream('./file2.txt');

// Instead of using data events, we use pipe
readableStream.pipe(writableStream);
```

Save this code and run `node index`. You'll see the file `file2.txt` created, with the same "Hello David Mark" content from `file.txt`. Simple, right?

One of the coolest things about pipes is that they return the destination stream. This allows us to chain them together, essentially creating a pipeline of data flowing from one stream to another. However, there's a catch: the destination stream must be readable, duplex, or a transform stream.

Let's illustrate this with another example. We'll use Node.js's built-in `zlib` module, which provides compression functionality using the gzip algorithm. In simple terms, `zlib` lets us create zipped files.

```
const fs = require('fs');
const zlib = require('zlib');

const readableStream = fs.createReadStream('./file.txt');
const gzip = zlib.createGzip(); // Create a gzip stream
const writableStream =
fs.createWriteStream('./file2.txt.gz');

readableStream.pipe(gzip).pipe(writableStream); //
Chaining pipes
```

Here, we first create a `readableStream` from `file.txt`. Then, we create a `gzip` stream using `zlib.createGzip()`. Finally, we create a `writableStream` that will write the compressed output to `file2.txt.gz`.

The magic happens when we chain the pipes: `readableStream.pipe(gzip).pipe(writableStream)`. We're effectively sending the data from the `readableStream` to the `gzip` stream for compression, and then the compressed data is piped to the `writableStream` to be written to the file.

Web Servers

We're diving into the **HTTP module**, a powerful tool that lets us create our very own web servers. But before we get into the code, let's take a moment to understand how the web works.

Imagine you're browsing the internet. You type a website address into your web browser, and suddenly, a page pops up filled with information. What's happening behind the scenes? Well, this is where the **client-server model** comes into play.

Your computer, with its web browser, is the **client**. It's requesting information from a **server**, a powerful computer that stores web pages and applications. When you type that URL, your browser sends a message to the server, saying, "Hey, I want to see this page!" The server then sends back a copy of the page, which is displayed on your browser.

But how do the client and server communicate? Here's where **HTTP** comes in. **HTTP stands for Hypertext Transfer Protocol**, and it's a set of rules that define the language used for communication between clients and servers. Think of it like a translator that ensures both sides understand each other.

The client sends an **HTTP request** to the server, asking for something. The server responds with an **HTTP response**, sending back the requested information, like a web page.

Now, where does Node.js fit into all of this? Node.js, with its asynchronous event loop and powerful networking capabilities, is perfect for creating **web servers** that can efficiently handle multiple requests at the same time. And the **HTTP module** is Node.js's way of interacting with this protocol, allowing us to create servers that can communicate over HTTP.

Creating a Node Server

First things first, we need to import the `http` module. We do this with the `require` function. Think of it like grabbing a tool from your toolbox:

```
const http = require('http');
```

Next, we'll use the `createServer` method to create our server. This method takes a callback function as an argument, which will be executed whenever a request is made to our server:

```
const server = http.createServer((request, response) => {
  // This is where we handle the request and build the
  response
});
```

The callback function gets two arguments: `request` and `response`. The `request` object contains information about the incoming request, and the `response` object is used to send back a response to the client. We'll explore these objects in more detail later.

Now, we'll use the `response` object to send back a simple "Hello World" message:

```
response.writeHead(200, { 'Content-Type':
'text/plain' });
response.end('Hello World!');
```

The `writeHead` method sets the HTTP status code (200 for success) and the content type (plain text in this case). The end method sends the response to the client.

Finally, we tell our server to listen for incoming requests on a specific port. We'll use port 3000:

```
const http = require('http');
const server = http.createServer((request, response) => {
  // This is where we handle the request and build the
  response
response.writeHead(200, { 'Content-Type':
'text/plain' });
response.end('Hello World!');
});
server.listen(3000, () => {
  console.log('Server running on port 3000');
});
```

Think of the port number like a door number in an apartment building. It tells the computer which server to connect to.

Now, let's run our code by typing node index.js in the terminal. You should see the message "Server running on port 3000" printed in your terminal.

To test our server, open your web browser and go to http://localhost:3000. You should see the "Hello World" message displayed on your screen!

Exercise: Let's try logging the request object to the console to see what information is available to us:

```
const http = require('http');

const server = http.createServer((request, response) => {
  console.log(request);

  response.writeHead(200, { 'Content-Type':
'text/plain' });
  response.end('Hello World!');
});

server.listen(3000, () => {
  console.log('Server running on port 3000');
});
```

Run the code and you'll see a lot of information about the request being logged to the terminal.

JSON Response

Let's imagine we want to send data about a superhero. We can create an object in our Node.js code and then send it as a JSON response.

```javascript
const http = require('http');

const server = http.createServer((req, res) => {
  // Create an object with superhero information
  const superhero = {
    firstName: 'Bruce',
    lastName: 'Wayne',
  };

  // Convert the object to JSON string
  const jsonData = JSON.stringify(superhero);

  // Set the content type header to indicate JSON data
  res.setHeader('Content-Type', 'application/json');

  // Send the JSON data as a response
  res.end(jsonData);
});

server.listen(3000, () => {
  console.log('Server listening on port 3000');
});
```

Run this code in your terminal with `node index.js` and then visit `http://localhost:3000` in your browser. You'll see a string representation of our superhero object.

Why does it look like a string? Well, to send data over the internet, we need to convert it to a format that both the server and the client can understand. JSON (JavaScript Object Notation) is perfect for this!

In our code, `JSON.stringify()` converts the JavaScript object to a JSON string. This JSON string is then sent as a response to the client. The client can then use `JSON.parse()` to convert this string back into a JavaScript object.

This is how you send JSON responses in Node.js. You've just built a simple API! This API, hosted at `localhost:3000`, can be accessed by other applications, including browsers, to get the superhero data.

We'll delve deeper into APIs and their design with Node.js in later lessons. For now, remember that setting the `Content-Type` header to `application/json` and using `JSON.stringify` are crucial for sending JSON responses to clients.

In the next lesson, we'll explore how to send HTML as a response from our server.

HTML Response

Let's send HTML as a response. Let's start by going back to our basic plain text response. Remember this code?

```
const http = require('http');

const server = http.createServer((req, res) => {
  res.writeHead(200, { 'Content-Type': 'text/plain' });
  res.end('Hello World!');
});

server.listen(3000, () => {
  console.log('Server listening on port 3000');
});
```

This code simply sends the text "Hello World!" to the browser.

Now, let's try to add some HTML to make our response more exciting. We'll wrap our "Hello World" text with an `<h1>` tag.

```
const http = require('http');

const server = http.createServer((req, res) => {
  res.writeHead(200, { 'Content-Type': 'text/plain' });
  res.end('<h1>Hello World!</h1>');
});

server.listen(3000, () => {
  console.log('Server listening on port 3000');
});
```

If we restart the server and refresh the browser, we'll see that the output doesn't change. It still displays as plain text. The reason is that we're telling the browser to treat the response as plain text with `'Content-Type': 'text/plain'`. To make the browser understand it's HTML, we need to change our `Content-Type` to `'text/html'`.

```
const http = require('http');

const server = http.createServer((req, res) => {
  res.writeHead(200, { 'Content-Type': 'text/html' });
  res.end('<h1>Hello World!</h1>');
});

server.listen(3000, () => {
  console.log('Server listening on port 3000');
});
```

Now, when we refresh the browser, our text will be bigger and bolder, which is the default style for an <h1> tag. This is how you send HTML content as a response!

But wait, there's more! Instead of building the HTML as a string in our JavaScript code, it's better to create a separate HTML file and send that content as a response. Let's create a new file called index.html and add this simple HTML code:

```
<!DOCTYPE html>
<html lang="en">
<head>
  <meta charset="UTF-8">
  <meta name="viewport" content="width=device-width,
initial-scale=1.0">
  <title>My HTML Response</title>
</head>
<body>
  <h1>Hello World!</h1>
</body>
</html>
```

Now, we need to read the contents of this file and send them back to the browser. We can use the `fs` module to read files.

```
const http = require('http');
const fs = require('fs');

const server = http.createServer((req, res) => {
  const html = fs.readFileSync('./index.html', 'utf-8');
  res.writeHead(200, { 'Content-Type': 'text/html' });
  res.end(html);
});

server.listen(3000, () => {
```

```
  console.log('Server listening on port 3000');
});
```

We use `fs.readFileSync` to read the entire contents of `index.html` and store them in the `html` variable. We then send this `html` content as a response. Now, when you refresh your browser, you should see the same `<h1>Hello World!</h1>` output, but it's coming from our separate `index.html` file!

You might be thinking, "That's cool, but what if my HTML file is huge? Reading the entire file at once could be inefficient." You're absolutely right! We can make our code more efficient and memory-friendly by using streams. We've already learned about streams, and we can use them here too. Let's modify our code to use a stream:

```
const http = require('http');
const fs = require('fs');

const server = http.createServer((req, res) => {
  const readStream = fs.createReadStream('./index.html',
'utf-8');
  res.writeHead(200, { 'Content-Type': 'text/html' });
  readStream.pipe(res);
});

server.listen(3000, () => {
  console.log('Server listening on port 3000');
});
```

Instead of reading the entire file into memory, we create a read stream with `fs.createReadStream` and pipe it directly to the response. This way, the browser receives the HTML content as it's read, making our code more efficient.

One more important thing: It's good practice to use `__dirname` (which represents the directory where your Node.js file is located) when referencing files. It helps maintain consistency and makes your code more portable. So, let's update our `fs.createReadStream` line:

```
const readStream = fs.createReadStream(__dirname +
'/index.html', 'utf-8');
```

Remember, this is just a basic example. You can add any HTML content and CSS styles to your `index.html` file, and your Node.js server will send it as a response.

The `'Content-Type': 'text/html'` header is essential for the browser to understand that it's receiving HTML content.

HTML Templates

In our previous lessons, we learned how to send HTML responses by reading a file and piping it to the response. This works great for static HTML pages where the content doesn't change. But what if we want to add dynamic values to our HTML? For example, displaying a logged-in user's name.

This is where HTML templates come in. We'll use a basic approach called string replacement to dynamically insert values into our HTML.

Let's break it down step-by-step.

1. Setting up our Template

First, we need a basic HTML template with a placeholder for our dynamic value. Create a file called `index.html` with the following content:

```
<!DOCTYPE html>
<html lang="en">
<head>
    <meta charset="UTF-8">
    <meta name="viewport" content="width=device-width,
initial-scale=1.0">
    <title>Node.js HTML Template</title>
</head>
<body>
    <h1>Hello {{ name }} welcome to Node!</h1>
</body>
</html>
```

This HTML file contains a `<h1>` tag with `{{ name }}` as a placeholder. We'll replace this placeholder with our actual name in the JavaScript code.

2. JavaScript Code

Now let's update our `index.js` file to handle the dynamic content injection.

```
const http = require('http');
```

```
const fs = require('fs');

const hostname = '127.0.0.1';
const port = 3000;

const server = http.createServer((req, res) => {
  res.statusCode = 200;
  res.setHeader('Content-Type', 'text/html');

  const name = 'David'; // This is the dynamic value

  let html = fs.readFileSync('index.html', 'utf-8'); //
Read the file contents
  html = html.replace('{{ name }}', name); // Replace the
placeholder

  res.end(html); // Send the updated HTML as response
});

server.listen(port, hostname, () => {
  console.log(`Server running at http://${hostname}:$
{port}/`);
});
```

In the code above, we:

- Read the HTML file using `fs.readFileSync()`.
- Store the file content in the `html` variable.
- Replace the `{{ name }}` placeholder with the `name` variable using the `replace()` method.
- Finally, send the updated HTML as a response.

3. Run the Code and See the Output

Save both files (`index.html` and `index.js`) and run your Node.js server. Open your web browser and navigate to `http://localhost:3000/`. You should see the output:

"Hello David welcome to Node!"

HTTP Routing

Imagine you're building a website. You want different pages for different content, right? Like, going to `/about` should show an "About Us" page, and going to `/api` could give you some data.

Let's see how to do this with our trusty HTTP module.

Currently, if you go to `localhost:3000`, you'll see the same message no matter where you go (`/about`, `/api`, etc.). This isn't how real websites work! We need to make our server respond differently depending on the URL.

First, let's get our hands dirty with a little experiment. The `request.url` property gives us the URL that the user requested. We're going to send that back to the browser to see what it looks like.

```javascript
const http = require('http');

const server = http.createServer((req, res) => {
  res.end(req.url);
});

server.listen(3000, () => {
  console.log('Server listening on port 3000');
});
```

Now, start your server and open your browser to `localhost:3000`. Try different URLs like `/about`, `/api`, and `/something-else`. See how the server sends back the URL you requested?

Now, let's use `request.url` to create different responses:

```javascript
const http = require('http');

const server = http.createServer((req, res) => {
  if (req.url === '/') { // Root path
    res.writeHead(200, { 'Content-Type': 'text/plain' });
    res.end('Home page');
  } else if (req.url === '/about') { // About page
    res.writeHead(200, { 'Content-Type': 'text/plain' });
    res.end('About page');
  } else if (req.url === '/api') { // API endpoint
    res.writeHead(200, { 'Content-Type':
'application/json' });
    res.end(JSON.stringify({ firstName: 'Bruce',
lastName: 'Wayne' }));
  } else { // Not found
    res.writeHead(404, { 'Content-Type': 'text/plain' });
    res.end('Page not found');
  }
});
```

```
server.listen(3000, () => {
  console.log('Server listening on port 3000');
});
```

Restart your server and check it out! Navigate to different URLs – you'll see the customized responses!

This is a basic example of routing. In real-world applications, you usually rely on frameworks like Express.js to handle this complex routing and much more.

Web Framework

We've learned about the HTTP module, how to create a server, access request information, send responses, modify headers, set response status codes, respond with plain text, HTML, and even JSON. We've even explored routing requests to different responses.

But here's the thing: while all that works great for smaller projects, building large-scale applications in this way would be a real pain. Imagine writing all that code for each request! That's where web frameworks come in.

Think of a web framework like a set of tools that simplify your life. They handle a lot of the boilerplate code and let you focus on the unique logic of your application. Frameworks like Angular, React, and Vue help build user interfaces without needing to deal with the low-level DOM API. Node.js has its own set of frameworks like Express, Nest, Koa, and Fastify. These frameworks build on top of the HTTP module, making it super easy to implement all the features we've learned about. Express is a very popular choice.

Before we move on to our next lesson, let's recap what we've learned about built-in modules:
- **Path Module:** Helps manage file and directory paths.
- **Events Module:** Introduces the concept of events and listeners.
- **Streams and Buffers:** Efficiently handle data in chunks.
- **File System (fs) Module:** Allows you to interact with the file system.
- **HTTP Module:** The foundation for creating servers and handling requests.

These are some of the most crucial modules to understand when learning Node.js. They provide the building blocks for all sorts of exciting projects.

libuv

Now we're going to take a peek under the hood of Node.js and explore libuv, the engine that makes Node's magic happen. We'll break it down into the "what," "why," and "how" of libuv.

What is libuv?

Imagine libuv as the unsung hero behind Node.js. It's a powerful cross-platform library written in C, and it's responsible for handling all those amazing asynchronous tasks Node.js can do. Think of it like the backstage crew for a smooth-running show.

Why do we need libuv?

Remember how Node.js loves to handle multiple tasks at the same time, making it super efficient? Well, that's where libuv comes in. It takes care of the heavy lifting of communicating with the operating system, making sure your code runs smoothly without blocking.

How does libuv work?

LibUv manages these asynchronous tasks using two key features: the **thread pool** and the **event loop**. It's like a well-coordinated team working together.

- **Thread Pool:** Picture the thread pool as a group of workers dedicated to handling specific tasks. They are the muscle behind the scenes, doing the heavy lifting.
- **Event Loop:** Think of the event loop as the conductor, constantly checking for any completed tasks and notifying the appropriate code to handle the result. It's the brains of the operation, making sure everything stays in sync.

We'll be diving deep into these two features in the next lesson.

Thread Pool

Let's start with something familiar: reading from a file using the `fs` module. Here's the code that reads contents from a file named "file.txt":

```
const fs = require('fs');

fs.readFile('file.txt', (err, data) => {
  if (err) {
    console.error(err);
    return;
  }
  console.log(data.toString());
});

console.log('first');
console.log('last');
```

When you run `node index.js`, you'll see "first", "last", and then the file's contents. This clearly shows that the `readFile` method is asynchronous and non-blocking, allowing the execution of code further down the line while the file contents are being read. But how does Node.js achieve this?

The answer lies in Libuv's thread pool. Imagine a conversation between JavaScript's main thread and Libuv:

- **Main thread:** "Hey Libuv, I need to read file contents, but that's a time-consuming task. I don't want to block other code from running. Can I offload this task to you?"
- **Libuv:** "Sure, main thread! Unlike you who are single-threaded, I have a pool of threads that I can use to handle these time-consuming tasks. Once the task is complete, I'll send the file contents back and the associated callback function will be executed."

So, Libuv's thread pool, as its name suggests, is a pool of threads that Node.js uses to offload time-consuming tasks, ensuring that the main thread isn't blocked for extended periods.

Go back to VS Code and explore the thread pool in more detail. We'll execute a method and measure its execution time in different scenarios, shedding light on what happens behind the scenes.

We'll use the `crypto` module for our experiments. This module provides cryptographic functionality and, like the `fs` module, utilizes Libuv's thread pool for some of its methods. We'll use the `pbkdf2` method, which stands for Password-Based Key Derivation Function 2. It's a popular method for hashing passwords before storing them. Don't worry about the details of the method or its arguments; just remember it's a CPU-intensive method that takes a long time and is offloaded to Libuv's thread pool.

Experiment 1:

We'll measure the time taken to run the synchronous version of `pbkdf2`. Here's the code:

```
const crypto = require('crypto');

const maxCalls = 3; // Adjust this value
const start = Date.now();

for (let i = 0; i < maxCalls; i++) {

    const password = crypto.pbkdf2Sync('password',
'salt', 100000, 64,    'sha512');

}
const end = Date.now();
console.log(`Password hashed in ${end - start}
milliseconds`);
```

When you run this code, you'll see the password hashed in a certain amount of time, which may vary depending on your hardware. Now, increase the maxCalls and run the code again. You'll notice that the time taken almost doubles.

This indicates that each call to `pbkdf2Sync` is synchronous and blocking. The execution happens sequentially, one after the other. In essence, any Node.js method with the "Sync" suffix runs on the main thread and blocks its execution. This is our inference from Experiment 1.

Experiment 2:

Now, let's invoke the asynchronous version of `pbkdf2`:

```
const crypto = require('crypto');

const maxCalls = 3; // Adjust this value
```

```
const start = Date.now();

for (let i = 0; i < maxCalls; i++) {

  crypto.pbkdf2('password', 'salt', 100000, 64, 'sha512',
(err, derivedKey) => {
    if (err) {
      console.error(err);
      return;
    }


  });
}
const end = Date.now();
console.log(`Password hashed in ${end - start}
milliseconds`);
```

We're calling pbkdf2 asynchronously within a loop that runs a specified number of times controlled by the maxCalls constant. The callback function is executed when the hashing is complete, logging the time taken.

When you run the code with maxCalls set to 1, you'll see a similar time to the synchronous version. However, when you increase maxCalls to 2 or 3, the total time taken doesn't increase proportionally. The second and third calls don't take twice or three times as long as the first call.

This suggests that each call to pbkdf2 is running on a separate thread within Libuv's thread pool. Although the operations are performed synchronously within their respective threads, from the perspective of the main thread, they appear asynchronous. This is our inference from Experiment 2.

Now you have a better understanding of how asynchronous methods are executed under the hood. But we're not done yet! There's more to uncover about the thread pool.

Thread Pool Size

In the previous lesson, we learned about libuv's thread pool and how the main thread offloads some of the asynchronous methods, like `pbkdf2`, into the thread pool. We saw that running `pbkdf2` three times resulted in parallel execution, hinting at at least three threads in the pool. But the question remains: how many threads are there in total? Let's find out with our next experiment.

Experiment 3

In this experiment, we'll change the number of `pbkdf2` calls to figure out the thread pool's size. We'll start by setting `maxCalls` to 4. Run the `node index.js` script a few times, and you'll notice that all four hashers complete in nearly the same amount of time, around 300 milliseconds.

Now, let's change `maxCalls` to 5. Run the script again, and something interesting happens. Hash 5 takes almost twice as long to complete compared to the first four! This indicates that libuv's thread pool has four threads.

The first four `pbkdf2` calls each get their own thread and complete quickly. However, the fifth call must wait for a thread to become available. When hash 1 finishes, hash 5 runs on that freed thread, resulting in a longer execution time.

Therefore, our inference from experiment 3 is that libuv's thread pool has four threads by default.

Experiment 4:

You might be wondering if we can increase the number of threads in the pool to improve performance by running more `pbkdf2` calls in parallel. The answer is yes!

To change the thread pool size, we need to set a process environment variable: `process.env.UV_THREADPOOL_SIZE`.

Let's try setting it to 5:

```
process.env.UV_THREADPOOL_SIZE = 5;
```

Now, rerun the script with `maxCalls` set to 5. You'll see that the fifth hash now takes almost the same time as the others.

Let's increase `maxCalls` to 6. The sixth hash takes twice as long. Finally, set the thread pool size to 6:

```
process.env.UV_THREADPOOL_SIZE = 6;
```

Now, the sixth hash no longer takes twice the time. By increasing the thread pool size, we've improved the overall execution time for multiple `pbkdf2` calls.

Therefore, our inference from experiment 4 is that we can improve performance by increasing the thread pool size.

Experiment 5: The Limits of Thread Pool Size

There's a crucial point to remember when increasing the thread pool size: if you go beyond the number of CPU cores on your machine, the average time taken per method execution can actually increase! Let's see why.

For experiment 5, let's change the thread pool size to 8 and `maxCalls` to 8. Rerunning the script shows that all eight hashes take around 300 milliseconds each.

Now, let's crank up the thread pool size to 16 and `maxCalls` to 16. This time, all 16 hashes take around 550-600 milliseconds, roughly double the previous execution time.

What's happening? My MacBook has eight CPU cores. The operating system has to juggle 16 threads across these eight cores.

Imagine it like this:

- **One** `pbkdf2` **call**: Takes one thread, which uses one CPU core, and completes in 270 milliseconds.
- **Eight** `pbkdf2` **calls**: Each call uses one thread, resulting in eight threads using eight cores, and still takes around 270 milliseconds per call.
- **Sixteen** `pbkdf2` **calls**: Sixteen threads need to share eight cores. The operating system switches between these threads to give each a fair amount of time. This "juggling" slows down the process, resulting in a longer execution time.

Therefore, our inference from experiment 5 is that increasing the thread pool size can help performance, but this is limited by the number of available CPU cores.

Now you have a better understanding of how libuv's thread pool helps execute asynchronous methods in Node.js. Remember, not all async methods are offloaded to the thread pool, which we'll explore in the next lesson!

Network I/O

Imagine you're browsing the web. You click a link, and your computer sends a request to a server somewhere on the internet. That request, and the server's response, are examples of network I/O. In Node.js, network I/O operations are handled differently compared to CPU-intensive tasks like encryption.

Let's see this in action with a little experiment. We're going to use the `https` module, a secure version of the familiar `http` module, and make a request to Google. Take a look at this code snippet:

```
const https = require('https');

function makeRequest() {
  const start = Date.now();
  https.request('https://www.google.com', (res) => {
    let data = '';
    res.on('data', (chunk) => {
      data += chunk;
    });
    res.on('end', () => {
      console.log(`Request completed in ${Date.now() -
start}ms`);
    });
  }).end();
}

for (let i = 0; i < 12; i++) {
  makeRequest();
}
```

In this code, we're making multiple requests to Google within a loop. We're tracking the time taken for each request and logging it to the console. Now, let's run this code with different values for `max_old_space_size`, a setting that influences the number of threads available.

First, try running the code with `max_old_space_size` set to 1. You'll likely see that each request takes around 200 milliseconds. Now, increase the `max_old_space_size` to 4, then 6, and finally 12. Notice anything interesting? The average time for each request stays roughly the same! Even with 12 concurrent requests, it's still around 200 to 300 milliseconds.

This is a critical observation. Why doesn't the request time increase as we increase the number of threads? Remember, we saw that CPU-intensive tasks can benefit from more threads. But, in this case, network I/O operations are handled differently.

Key Takeaways:

- **Network I/O and the Thread Pool:** Unlike CPU-bound operations, network I/O operations don't directly rely on the thread pool.

- **Operating System's Role:** Node.js delegates network I/O tasks to the operating system's kernel. This kernel handles the communication with the network and manages these operations.
- **Asynchronous Nature:** Node.js uses asynchronous mechanisms to manage network I/O, allowing the main thread to continue executing other tasks while waiting for responses from the network.

Think of it like this: Instead of waiting for the barista to make your coffee, you order it and continue browsing the shop while you wait. When the coffee is ready, you get a notification. That's similar to how Node.js handles network I/O. The main thread continues working, and the operating system tells Node.js when the response is ready.

Exercise:

Modify the code above to make requests to different websites (like Facebook, Twitter, or your favorite news site) and see if the time taken for each request varies significantly.

Understanding the Code:

- `https.request`: This function makes an HTTPS request to the specified URL.
- `res.on('data')`: This event listener is triggered whenever a chunk of data is received from the server.
- `res.on('end')`: This event listener is triggered when the response is fully received.

Node.js's use of the operating system kernel for network I/O makes it very efficient. It can handle numerous simultaneous network connections without slowing down the main thread.

In our next lesson, we'll delve into more advanced concepts related to asynchronous programming in Node.js.

Event Loop

This mysterious but crucial component is responsible for handling the execution of asynchronous code.

Let's refresh our memory on async code. JavaScript, at its core, is synchronous and single-threaded. This means it executes code line by line, and only one task can be running at a time. To achieve asynchronous behavior, Node.js relies heavily on libuv, a library that helps manage asynchronous operations.

Imagine the Node.js runtime as a two-part machine:

- **The V8 Engine:** This engine executes your JavaScript code. It has a **heap** where variables and functions are stored and a **call stack** where functions are pushed and popped during execution. This is a Last-In-First-Out (LIFO) data structure.
- **Libuv:** This library handles asynchronous tasks, like reading files or making network requests. Libuv interacts with the operating system to run these tasks efficiently without blocking the main thread of execution.

Let's illustrate this with some code snippets:

Synchronous Code Execution

```
console.log("First");
console.log("Second");
console.log("Third");
```

Here's how this code runs:

- The global function (our main entry point) is pushed onto the call stack.
- `console.log("First")` is pushed, executed, and popped off the stack.
- `console.log("Second")` is pushed, executed, and popped off the stack.
- `console.log("Third")` is pushed, executed, and popped off the

stack.
- Finally, the global function is popped off the stack, and the execution is complete.

Asynchronous Code Execution

```
console.log("First");
fs.readFile("myFile.txt", (err, data) => {
  console.log("Second");
});
console.log("Third");
```

In this example, `fs.readFile` is asynchronous. Here's how the flow works:

- The global function is pushed onto the call stack.
- `console.log("First")` is pushed, executed, and popped off the stack.
- `fs.readFile("myFile.txt", (err, data) =>` `{ console.log("Second"); })` is pushed onto the stack. Since `fs.readFile` is asynchronous, it's offloaded to libuv, and the callback function (`(err, data) =>` `{ console.log("Second"); })` is passed to libuv.
- The `fs.readFile` function is popped off the stack as its job is done.
- `console.log("Third")` is pushed, executed, and popped off the stack.
- Now, the call stack is empty.
- Libuv, in the background, reads the file. Once the file reading is complete, the callback function is pushed back onto the call stack, "Second" is logged, and the callback is popped off the stack.
- The global function is popped off the stack.

You might be thinking, "How does Node.js know when to execute those callback functions?" This is where the **event loop** comes into play.

Think of the event loop as the conductor of your Node.js symphony. It orchestrates the execution of all your code, both synchronous and asynchronous. It continually checks different queues for callbacks that are ready to be executed.

Here's a visual representation of the event loop:

The event loop six queues:

- **Micro Task Queues:** These include the **Next Tick Queue** and **Promise Queue**. They have the highest priority. Callbacks associated with `process.nextTick()` and JavaScript promises are stored here.
- **Timer Queue:** This queue holds callbacks for `setTimeout()` and `setInterval()`.
- **I/O Queue:** This queue is responsible for all the asynchronous I/O operations we discussed earlier.
- **Check Queue:** This queue contains callbacks for `setImmediate()`, a Node.js-specific function for scheduling callbacks to be run after the current event loop iteration.
- **Close Queue:** This queue holds callbacks associated with the close events of asynchronous tasks.

The event loop works in a continuous cycle:

- **Execute the call stack:** If the call stack is not empty, it executes the code on the stack.
- **Check microtask queues:** The event loop first checks if there are any pending tasks in the Next Tick Queue and then in the Promise Queue. If any are present, they are executed.
- **Check timer queue:** The event loop then checks the Timer Queue for any tasks that are ready to be executed based on their timeout.
- **Check I/O Queue:** If any I/O operations have completed, the event loop moves the corresponding callback to the call stack.
- **Check Check Queue:** The event loop checks the Check Queue for tasks that are ready to run.
- **Check Close Queue:** The event loop checks the Close Queue for close events.
- **Repeat:** The event loop continues this cycle until there are no more tasks to execute.

The event loop is the core of Node.js's asynchronous programming model. It ensures that your code executes efficiently and in a non-blocking manner. By understanding its workings, you can write more robust and performant Node.js applications.

Microtask Queues

In the last lesson, we explored the Event Loop in Node.js and built a mental model of how asynchronous code runs. We learned that the Event Loop has six queues: two microtask queues (the 'next tick' queue and the 'promise' queue), a timer queue, an I/O queue, a check queue, and a close queue. In each loop, callback functions are dequeued when appropriate and executed on the call stack.

To really understand the order of execution for asynchronous methods in Node.js, let's dive into some code examples. These experiments will help you get a better grasp of how things work, just like how learning about a thread pool involves hands-on practice.

We'll focus on the two microtask queues for our first set of experiments. Before we begin, let's learn how to add callback functions to these queues:

- **Next Tick Queue:** To queue a callback into the next tick queue, we use the built-in `process.nextTick()` method. The syntax is straightforward:

```
process.nextTick(() => {
    // Your callback function goes here
});
```

When `process.nextTick()` is executed on the call stack, the passed-in callback function is queued in the next tick queue.

- **Promise Queue:** We can queue callbacks into the promise queue in various ways, but for our experiments, we'll use `Promise.resolve().then()`:

```
Promise.resolve().then(() => {
    // Your callback function goes here
});
```

When the promise resolves, the function passed to the `then()` block will be queued in the promise queue.

Now that we understand how to add functions to the microtask queues, let's start with our first experiment.

Create an empty `index.js` file. Inside it, let's write the following code:

```
console.log('1');
console.log('2');

process.nextTick(() => {
    console.log('This is process.nextTick 1');
});
```

Think about what the output might be before running the code.

If you run `node index.js`, you'll see the following output:

```
1
2
This is process.nextTick 1
```

In Node.js, user-written synchronous JavaScript code takes priority over asynchronous code that the runtime intends to execute later. In our experiment, the two `console.log` statements are executed before the callback function passed to `process.nextTick()`.

Order of execution:

- `console.log('1')` is pushed onto the call stack, logs the message, and is popped off the stack.
- `console.log('2')` is pushed onto the call stack, logs the message, and is popped off the stack.
- `process.nextTick()` is executed, queues the callback function in the next tick queue, and is popped off the stack.
- No more user-written synchronous code to execute, so control enters the Event Loop.
- The callback function from the next tick queue is dequeued, pushed onto the stack, logs its message, and is popped off the stack.

Let's move on to our second experiment. Comment out the code from the first experiment and start fresh:

```
Promise.resolve().then(() => {
    console.log('This is Promise.resolve 1');
});

process.nextTick(() => {
    console.log('This is process.nextTick 1');
});
```

Again, pause for a moment and predict the output before running the code.

Running `node index.js` will give us:

```
This is process.nextTick 1
This is Promise.resolve 1
```

All callbacks in the next tick queue are executed before callbacks in the promise queue.

Order of execution:

- The call stack executes line 1, queuing the `console.log` function in the promise queue.
- The call stack executes line 2, queuing the callback function in the next tick queue.
- No more user-written code, so control enters the Event Loop.
- The next tick queue has priority, and its callback function is executed, logging the message.
- The promise queue callback function is executed, logging its message.

Let's explore a more complex version of the second experiment:

```
process.nextTick(() => {
    console.log('This is process.nextTick 1');
});

process.nextTick(() => {
    console.log('This is process.nextTick 2');
    process.nextTick(() => {
        console.log('This is the inner nextTick inside
nextTick');
    });
});

Promise.resolve().then(() => {
    console.log('This is Promise.resolve 1');
});

Promise.resolve().then(() => {
    console.log('This is Promise.resolve 2');
    process.nextTick(() => {
        console.log('This is the inner nextTick inside
Promise');
    });
});

Promise.resolve().then(() => {
    console.log('This is Promise.resolve 3');
});
```

Pause and try to figure out the execution order!

The output when you run `node index.js` is:

```
This is process.nextTick 1
This is process.nextTick 2
```

```
This is the inner nextTick inside nextTick
This is Promise.resolve 1
This is Promise.resolve 2
This is Promise.resolve 3
This is the inner nextTick inside Promise
```

Order of execution:

- All six `process.nextTick` and `Promise.resolve` calls are executed on the call stack, queuing their respective callbacks.
- The Event Loop takes over, prioritizing the next tick queue.
- The next tick callbacks are executed in order, with the second callback adding an inner next tick callback to the end of the queue.
- Once the next tick queue is empty, the promise queue is processed. The second promise callback also adds an inner next tick callback to the next tick queue, but the Event Loop continues processing the promise queue.
- The next tick queue is processed again, executing the inner next tick callbacks.

Important Note:

While `process.nextTick()` can be useful, be cautious of its overuse, as it can cause the Event Loop to become "starved." If you continuously call `process.nextTick()`, control might never move beyond the microtask queues, preventing other queues from processing their tasks. The official Node.js documentation recommends using `process.nextTick()` primarily for error handling, cleanup, or retries.

Timer Queue

Before we start experimenting, let me introduce the tools we'll use to queue callback functions into the Timer Queue: `setTimeout` and `setInterval`. For the rest of this book, we'll focus on `setTimeout`. Here's the syntax for your reference:

```
setTimeout(callbackFunction, delay);
```

The first argument is the callback function you want to execute, and the second argument specifies the delay in milliseconds before the function is called.

Let's jump into our next experiment. We'll queue tasks in both microtask queues and the Timer Queue. Building upon our previous code, we'll add three calls to `setTimeout`, each with a delay of 0 milliseconds. This means the callbacks will be queued as soon as the `setTimeout` statement is executed on the call stack.

```
setTimeout(() => {
  console.log('setTimeout 1');
}, 0);

setTimeout(() => {
  console.log('setTimeout 2');
}, 0);

setTimeout(() => {
  console.log('setTimeout 3');
}, 0);

process.nextTick(() => {
  console.log('process.nextTick 1');
});

process.nextTick(() => {
  console.log('process.nextTick 2');
});

process.nextTick(() => {
  console.log('process.nextTick 3');
});

Promise.resolve().then(() => {
  console.log('Promise 1');
});

Promise.resolve().then(() => {
  console.log('Promise 2');
});

Promise.resolve().then(() => {
  console.log('Promise 3');
});


// Output:
// process.nextTick 1
// process.nextTick 2
// process.nextTick 3
// Promise 1
// Promise 2
```

```
// Promise 3
// setTimeout 1
// setTimeout 2
// setTimeout 3
```

Take a moment to analyze the output. Can you figure out the order of execution?

From this experiment, we can infer that **callbacks in microtask queues are executed before callbacks in the Timer Queue**.

Let's move on to experiment number four. We'll modify the code from experiment three by slightly changing the callback function passed to the second `setTimeout` call:

```
setTimeout(() => {
  console.log('setTimeout 2');
  process.nextTick(() => {
    console.log('this is the inner nextTick inside
setTimeout');
  });
}, 0);
```

Pause for a moment and predict the output.

Run the code, and you'll notice that the output is almost identical to the previous experiment, except for the last part. This is because the `inner` `nextTick` callback inside `setTimeout` 2 is executed before the `setTimeout` 3 callback.

So, what does this tell us? **Callbacks in microtask queues are executed in between the execution of callbacks in the Timer Queue.**

Finally, we come to our fifth experiment. This time, we'll run three simple `setTimeout` statements with different delays: one second, 500 milliseconds, and zero seconds.

```
setTimeout(() => {
  console.log('setTimeout 1');
}, 1000);

setTimeout(() => {
  console.log('setTimeout 2');
}, 500);

setTimeout(() => {
  console.log('setTimeout 3');
```

```
}, 0);

// Output:
// setTimeout 3
// setTimeout 2
// setTimeout 1
```

Pause and try to understand the output. It's a bit straightforward, since it only involves the `Timer` queue.

The result is: `setTimeout` 3, followed by `setTimeout` 2, and finally `setTimeout` 1. This leads us to our final inference: **Timer Queue callbacks are executed in FIFO order (First In First Out).** The `setTimeout` callback with the least delay is queued up first and executed first by the event loop.

One important note: although we've been calling it a "queue," the Timer Queue is actually a **Min Heap data structure**. However, for our understanding, thinking of it as a queue simplifies the process.

I/O Queue

Let's start by understanding how to queue a callback function into the I/O. Many of the asynchronous methods from built-in Node.js modules queue their callback functions in the I/O. We'll use the `readFile` method from the `fs` module.

```
const fs = require('fs');

fs.readFile('./index.js', (err, data) => {
  console.log('This is readFile 1');
});

process.nextTick(() => {
  console.log('Next Tick');
});

Promise.resolve().then(() => {
  console.log('Promise Resolve');
});
```

Let's break down the code. We import the `fs` module first. Then, we call the `readFile` method with the path to our current file. We're not actually using the file contents, so we'll simply ignore the arguments in the callback function and just print a log message.

After `readFile`, we queue a callback in the next queue and another in the promise queue. Pretty simple, right?

Let's run `node index.js`

```
Next Tick
Promise Resolve
This is readFile 1
```

From the output, we can infer that callbacks in the microtask queue (next tick and promise queues) are executed before callbacks in the I/O.

Let's analyze this with the event loop:

- When the call stack executes all statements in our code snippet, we have one callback in the next queue, one in the promise queue, and one in the I/O.
- The event loop starts. The next queue has the highest priority, followed by the promise queue, then the I/O.
- The first callback from the next tick queue is dequeued and executed, logging its message to the console.
- The next queue is now empty, so the event loop moves to the promise queue. The callback is dequeued and executed, logging its message.
- The promise queue is empty, so the event loop moves to the timer queue. Since there are no callbacks in the timer queue, it moves to the I/O.
- The I/O callback is dequeued and executed, printing its final log message.

Here's a slightly different code snippet:

```
const fs = require('fs');

fs.readFile('./index.js', (err, data) => {
  console.log('This is readFile 1');
});

setTimeout(() => {
  console.log('Set Timeout 1');
}, 0);
```

This time, instead of queueing callbacks in the microtask queues, we're using `setTimeout` with a 0-second delay to queue a callback in the timer queue.

Let's run `node index`.

```
This is readFile 1
Set Timeout 1
```

This might not be the output you expected! Let's rerun `node index` a few times.

```
Set Timeout 1
This is readFile 1
```

Notice that the output isn't consistent. Sometimes `readFile` runs first, sometimes `setTimeout` runs first! You can always see 'Set Timeout' running first.

This inconsistent behavior is expected when you run the code multiple times on your computer. You simply can't guarantee that a `setTimeout` callback with a 0-millisecond delay will execute before the `readFile` callback.

Why does this happen?

The anomaly arises due to a minimum delay set for timers in Google Chrome. If you search "chromium dom timer C++ file", you'll find the C++ code for the DOM timer. Look for `DOMTimer::DOMTimer`. You'll see a calculation for the interval in milliseconds, with a maximum value of 1 millisecond or the user-specified interval multiplied by 1 millisecond. This means that if you pass 0 milliseconds, the interval is set to a maximum of 1, which is 1 millisecond.

Node.js follows a similar implementation. When you set a 0-millisecond delay, it gets overridden to a 1-millisecond delay. But how does this 1-millisecond delay affect the order of execution?

At the beginning of the event loop, Node.js checks if the 1-millisecond timer has elapsed. If the event loop enters the timer queue at 0.05 milliseconds, the 1-millisecond callback won't be ready yet, and the control moves to the I/O, executing the `readFile` callback. In the next iteration of the event loop, the timer queue callback will be executed.

However, if the CPU is busy and the event loop enters the timer queue at 1.01 milliseconds, the timer would have already elapsed, and the timer queue callback would be executed first, followed by the `readFile` callback in the I/O.

Because of this uncertainty in CPU utilization and the 0-millisecond delay being overwritten to 1 millisecond, we can never guarantee the order of execution between a 0-millisecond timer and an I/O callback.

For our final experiment, let's understand the order of execution of callbacks in the microtask queues, the timer queue, and the I/O combined.

Here's the code:

```
const fs = require('fs');

fs.readFile('./index.js', (err, data) => {
  console.log('This is readFile 1');
});

process.nextTick(() => {
  console.log('Next Tick');
});

Promise.resolve().then(() => {
  console.log('Promise Resolve');
});

setTimeout(() => {
  console.log('Set Timeout 1');
}, 0);

for (let i = 0; i < 10000000; i++) {
  // Do nothing
}
```

We have `readFile`, `process.nextTick`, `Promise.resolve`, and `setTimeout`. To avoid the timer issue from the last experiment, we've added a `for` loop that does nothing, ensuring that the timer has elapsed when the control reaches the timer queue.

Let's run `node index`.

```
Next Tick
Promise Resolve
Set Timeout 1
This is readFile 1
```

The output confirms that the next tick callback is executed first, followed by the promise callback, then the timer callback, and finally the I/O callback. We can infer that I/O callbacks are executed after microtask queue callbacks and timer queue callbacks.

The order of execution:

- The call stack executes all statements, resulting in one callback in each queue (next tick, promise, timer, and I/O).
- The event loop begins. The next tick queue's callback is dequeued and executed, logging its message.
- The promise queue's callback is dequeued and executed, logging its message.
- The timer queue's callback is dequeued and executed.
- Finally, the I/O callback is dequeued and executed, logging its final message.

That's pretty much it about the I/O and its priority in the event loop.

I/O Polling

In the last lesson, we explored how the I/O Queue (I/O) influences the order of execution in our Node.js programs. Now, we'll continue to dive deeper into the I/O, but also introduce the Check Queue, which plays a crucial role in managing our asynchronous operations.

Before we jump into our experiment, there's a key concept to understand: the `setImmediate()` function. This function allows us to queue callback functions into the Check Queue. It works similarly to `process.nextTick()`, where we simply pass in a callback function. Think of it like a waiting room after the main I/O waiting area – it holds functions that are ready to be executed, but only after the I/O operations are done.

Let's get our hands dirty with experiment number nine! We'll build upon the code from the previous lesson, which included a `readFile` callback, a `nextTick` callback, a Promise resolution callback, a `setTimeout` callback, and a `setImmediate` callback.

```
const fs = require('fs');

// readFile callback
fs.readFile('example.txt', (err, data) => {
  console.log('readFile 1', data.toString());
});
```

```
// nextTick callback
process.nextTick(() => {
  console.log('nextTick 1');
});

// promise resolution callback
new Promise((resolve, reject) => {
  resolve('promise 1');
}).then((data) => {
  console.log('promise 1', data);
});

// setTimeout callback
setTimeout(() => {
  console.log('setTimeout 1');
}, 0);

// setImmediate callback
setImmediate(() => {
  console.log('setImmediate 1');
});
```

Now, let's run this code and observe the output:

```
nextTick 1
promise 1 promise 1
setTimeout 1
setImmediate 1
readFile 1 example text
```

Notice something strange? `setImmediate 1` is printed *before* `readFile 1`, even though the Check Queue usually executes after the I/O. This is where the magic of I/O Polling comes in!

Think of the Event Loop as a busy worker. It checks the microtask queues (like `nextTick` and `Promise`) first, then moves to the timer queue, and finally reaches the I/O. You might expect the `readFile` callback to be present in the I/O, but it's not!

Here's why: the Event Loop *polls* the I/O operations. This means it checks if the I/O operations have finished and only adds the corresponding callbacks to the I/O *after* they're complete. So, when the Event Loop reaches the I/O, it's empty because the `readFile` operation is still in progress.

Instead, the Event Loop proceeds to the Check Queue, finds the setImmediate callback, and executes it. Now, the Event Loop starts a new iteration, and this time, the readFile callback is finally added to the I/O (since the file reading is done) and executed.

This explains the seemingly unexpected order of execution: setImmediate executes before readFile.

Exercise:

Try adding another setTimeout callback with a delay of 1000 milliseconds. Can you predict where it will appear in the output, considering the I/O Polling?

Solution:

```javascript
const fs = require('fs');

// readFile callback
fs.readFile('example.txt', (err, data) => {
  console.log('readFile 1', data.toString());
});

// nextTick callback
process.nextTick(() => {
  console.log('nextTick 1');
});

// promise resolution callback
new Promise((resolve, reject) => {
  resolve('promise 1');
}).then((data) => {
  console.log('promise 1', data);
});

// setTimeout callback
setTimeout(() => {
  console.log('setTimeout 1');
}, 0);

// setImmediate callback
setImmediate(() => {
  console.log('setImmediate 1');
});

// setTimeout callback with 1000ms delay
setTimeout(() => {
  console.log('setTimeout 2');
```

```
}, 1000);
```

The output will be:

```
nextTick 1
promise 1 promise 1
setTimeout 1
setImmediate 1
readFile 1 example text
(after 1 second)
setTimeout 2
```

The `setTimeout` with a delay of 1000 milliseconds will be executed last because its timer is set for 1 second.

In our next lesson, we'll delve into the Check Queue and explore its behavior in more detail.

Check Queue

We've been diving deep into the event loop in Node.js, and now we're going to focus on a specific part called the **check queue**. This queue plays a critical role in how Node.js manages your code's execution.

Let's imagine you're running a script with multiple asynchronous operations. These operations, like reading a file or making a network request, might take some time. While they're happening, your program doesn't just sit idle. It uses the **event loop** to manage these asynchronous tasks efficiently. The check queue is one of the key players in this process.

Think of the check queue as a waiting area for certain tasks. These tasks are specifically those triggered by events like timers (using `setTimeout`), `setImmediate`, and `process.nextTick`.

Let's start with an experiment to see how the check queue interacts with other queues. We'll put a `setImmediate` call inside the callback of a file reading operation:

```
const fs = require('fs');

fs.readFile('somefile.txt', (err, data) => {
  if (err) {
    console.error(err);
  } else {
```

```
    console.log('File contents:', data.toString());
    setImmediate(() => {
      console.log('This is inner setImmediate inside
readFile');
    });
  }
});
```

In this code, we're reading a file. After the file is read successfully, we call `setImmediate` to schedule a function to execute.

When you run this code, you'll notice the `setImmediate` callback executes *after* the file reading operation completes. This tells us that the check queue (where `setImmediate` callbacks reside) gets processed after the IO queue (where file reading callbacks live).

To understand this better, let's analyze how the event loop works in this scenario:

1. **Call Stack:** Your code starts executing on the call stack.
2. **IO Queue:** When `fs.readFile` is called, it triggers an asynchronous operation and gets added to the IO queue.
3. **Event Loop:** The event loop starts checking the queues.
4. **Next Tick Queue:** The event loop checks the next tick queue (for `process.nextTick` callbacks) first.
5. **Promise Queue:** Then it checks the promise queue (for promise callbacks).
6. **Timer Queue:** After that, it checks the timer queue (for `setTimeout` callbacks).
7. **IO Queue:** Finally, the event loop checks the IO queue.
8. **IO Operation Completion:** When the file read is finished, its callback gets executed from the IO queue.
9. **Check Queue:** Once the IO queue is empty, the event loop processes the check queue. This is where our `setImmediate` callback will be executed.

Let's explore another experiment. We'll add `process.nextTick` and `Promise.resolve` within the file reading callback:

```
const fs = require('fs');

fs.readFile('somefile.txt', (err, data) => {
  if (err) {
    console.error(err);
```

```
  } else {
    console.log('File contents:', data.toString());
    setImmediate(() => {
      console.log('This is inner setImmediate inside
readFile');
    });
    process.nextTick(() => {
      console.log('This is inner process.nextTick inside
readFile');
    });
    Promise.resolve().then(() => {
      console.log('This is inner Promise.resolve inside
readFile');
    });
  }
});
```

When you run this code, you'll notice:

`process.nextTick` and `Promise.resolve` execute *before* the `setImmediate` callback.

This confirms that both `process.nextTick` and `Promise.resolve` have higher priority than `setImmediate`. They are both considered **micro-tasks**, and Node.js prioritizes micro-tasks over check queue tasks.

Let's try a scenario with multiple `setImmediate` calls and a `process.nextTick` call:

```
const fs = require('fs');

setImmediate(() => {
  console.log('setImmediate 1');
});

setImmediate(() => {
  console.log('setImmediate 2');
  process.nextTick(() => {
    console.log('process.nextTick 1');
  });
  Promise.resolve().then(() => {
    console.log('Promise.resolve 1');
  });
});

setImmediate(() => {
  console.log('setImmediate 3');
```

```
});
```

In this experiment, you'll see:

The `process.nextTick` and `Promise.resolve` callbacks execute *in between* the second and third `setImmediate` callbacks.

This demonstrates that micro-tasks are executed *immediately* after each check queue task.

Finally, let's look at a bit of an anomaly:

```
const fs = require('fs');

setTimeout(() => {
  console.log('setTimeout 1');
}, 0);

setImmediate(() => {
  console.log('setImmediate 1');
});
```

In this example, you might see the `setImmediate` callback execute *before* the `setTimeout` callback, or vice versa. This is because `setTimeout` with a delay of 0 milliseconds is actually scheduled for the next event loop iteration. The order of execution isn't guaranteed in this case.

Exercise:

Try modifying the experiments by adding more calls to `setImmediate`, `process.nextTick`, or `Promise.resolve`. See if you can predict the order of execution based on what we've learned!

Understanding the check queue and how it interacts with other queues is essential for writing efficient and predictable Node.js code. Keep experimenting, and you'll gain a solid understanding of the event loop's inner workings!

Close Queue

 In this lesson, we're diving into the final queue in the Node.js Event Loop: the **Close Queue**. To understand it, we'll run the last experiment in this book.

```
const fs = require('fs');
```

```
const readableStream =
fs.createReadStream('your_file.txt');

readableStream.close();

readableStream.on('close', () => {
  console.log('This is from readable stream close event
callback');
});

setImmediate(() => {
  console.log('setImmediate');
});

setTimeout(() => {
  console.log('setTimeout');
}, 0);

Promise.resolve().then(() => {
  console.log('Promise.resolve');
});

process.nextTick(() => {
  console.log('process.nextTick');
});
```

Now, let's break it down step by step. We start by importing the `fs` module to work with files. Next, we create a readable stream using `fs.createReadStream`, which points to the file `your_file.txt`. We then close the stream with `readableStream.close()`. This triggers the 'close' event, which is essential for our experiment.

We attach a listener to this `close` event with `readableStream.on('close', ...)`. This listener is a callback function, and its output is "This is from readable stream close event callback".

Finally, we have our familiar methods: `setImmediate`, `setTimeout`, `Promise.resolve`, and `process.nextTick`. These are all methods we've explored in previous lessons.

Now, the big question: what order will these functions execute? Try to predict the output.

When you run the code using `node index.js`, you'll see the following order:

- process.nextTick
- Promise.resolve
- setTimeout
- setImmediate
- This is from readable stream close event callback

This experiment shows us that **Close Queue callbacks are executed after all other queues' callbacks within a single iteration of the event loop**.

Let's analyze this:

- The call stack executes all statements in your code.
- We end up with one callback in each queue (except the I/O queue, which is empty in this example).
- The event loop takes control.
- It first dequeues and executes the `process.nextTick` callback.
- Next, it executes the `Promise.resolve` callback.
- Then, it moves to the timer queue and executes the `setTimeout` callback.
- Finally, it executes the `setImmediate` callback.
- After all other queues are processed, the event loop finally reaches the Close Queue and executes the close event callback.

Simple, right? If you've followed along with our previous lessons about the Event Loop, you'll understand the pattern here.

Let's wrap up our Event Loop exploration with some key takeaways:

- The Event Loop is a core C program in Node.js. It manages both synchronous and asynchronous code execution.
- The Event Loop orchestrates callbacks in six distinct queues: `process.nextTick`, `Promise`, `Timer`, `I/O`, `Check`, and `Close`.
- The `process.nextTick` method queues callbacks into the `process.nextTick` queue.
- Resolving or rejecting a promise queues callbacks into the `Promise` queue.
- Using `setTimeout` or `setInterval` puts callbacks into the `Timer` queue.

- Asynchronous operations queue callbacks into the I/O queue.
- The setImmediate function queues callbacks into the Check queue.
- Finally, attaching listeners to close events (like we saw in our experiment) queues callbacks into the Close queue.

The order of execution always follows the same pattern, with process.nextTick and Promise queues executing between each queue and each callback within the Timer and Check queues.

We've completed our journey of understanding the Node.js Event Loop. I hope this book has helped you get a solid grasp on how asynchronous code works in Node.js.

What is npm?

In this lesson, we're going to dive into **npm**. You might be wondering, "What is npm?" Well, npm is two things: **The world's largest software library and a software package manager.** Let's break down those two points.

First, imagine a library full of books written by different authors. npm is like a library for code! It's a giant registry filled with code packages created by developers from around the globe. These packages are like pre-written building blocks that you can use in your projects. Imagine wanting to add a feature to your project like a fancy image slider, but you don't want to write all the code yourself. Instead, you can search for an image slider package on npm and easily add it to your project! This saves you time and effort.

Think of it like ordering a code package, then publishing it to the npm registry for other developers to use. On the other hand, you can find a package created by someone else that solves your problem and use it without having to build everything from scratch. You can explore these packages at **npmjs.com**, where you can search and discover a vast collection of JavaScript code.

Now, the second part - npm is also a **software package manager.** We've seen how developers share and use code packages, but there's a lot to consider when managing these packages within a project. For example, how do you publish a package? How do you download a package? What happens if the package author changes something?

How do you update a package you've already installed? What if your package needs another package to work? Managing packages in a project isn't as simple as it sounds.

Here's where npm, as a package manager, comes in handy. It provides a command-line interface (CLI) tool that helps you install, update, and manage packages in your project. We'll delve deeper into this CLI tool in the upcoming lessons. For now, the key takeaway is that npm makes managing packages much easier!

You might be wondering, "Do I need to install npm separately?" The answer is **no!** npm comes bundled with Node.js. To verify if npm is installed, open your terminal and run the command `npm -v`. You should see the version of npm installed on your machine.

It's also interesting to note that **npm initially stood for "Node Package Manager."** However, over time, npm has evolved and now manages packages for the JavaScript programming language in general, not just Node.js. That's why it's now simply "npm" (all lowercase).

So, why is learning about npm so important? Remember how I mentioned using code written by others? That's where npm comes in. Whether you're building a small side project or a large-scale application, you'll almost certainly rely on npm. It's a fundamental part of working with Node.js, which is why we're dedicating this lesson to understanding how to use it effectively.

package.json

 In the previous lesson, we learned about npm and why it's a crucial part of the Node.js ecosystem. Now, let's dive into our first concept within the npm universe: `package.json`.

What is `package.json`?

Think of `package.json` as npm's control center. It's a special JSON file that lives in the root directory of your project, holding all the essential information about your package. It's like a passport for your project, describing what it is, how to run it, and what dependencies it needs.

Why do we need `package.json`**?**

The `package.json` file is the backbone of npm's functionality. It allows the npm command-line interface (CLI) to understand and manage your project. It tells npm how to install, run, and publish your code.

Creating your first `package.json`

Let's get our hands dirty! We'll create a simple project with a `package.json` file.

1. **Create a folder:** Start by creating a new folder named "my-custom-package".

2. **Create an index.js file:** Inside the folder, create a file named "index.js". This will be our entry point.

3. **Write some code:** In `index.js`, add the following code:
   ```
   function greet(name) {
       console.log(`Hello ${name}, welcome to David
   Mark!`);
   }

   module.exports = greet;
   ```
   This code defines a simple function called `greet` that takes a name as an argument and logs a welcome message to the console.

4. **Create package.json:** Now, create a new file named "package.json" in the same folder.

5. **Start with curly braces:** Begin the file with empty curly braces {}, as it's a JSON file.

Let's populate `package.json`

There are many fields we can add to our `package.json` file, but let's focus on some key ones:

- `name`: This field defines the name of your package. It should be lowercase, one word, and can include hyphens or underscores. Let's use `"greet-david_mark"`.

- `version`: This field defines the current version of your package. It should follow semantic versioning guidelines (we'll explore that later!). For now, let's start with `"1.0.0"`.
- `description`: This field provides a brief description of your package. Let's use `"David Mark greeting package"`.
- `keywords`: This field is an array of strings, used for indexing your package on the npm registry. Let's add `"david_mark"` and `"greet"` to help users find our package.
- `main`: This field defines the entry point of your project. In our case, it's `"index.js"`.

Putting it all together:

Our `package.json` will look like this:

```
{
  "name": "greet-david_mark",
  "version": "1.0.0",
  "description": "David Mark greeting package",
  "keywords": [
    "david_mark",
    "greet"
  ],
  "main": "index.js"
}
```

Using `npm init` **to generate** `package.json`

While we manually created our `package.json` file, you don't have to do this every time. The `npm init` command is your friend!

- **Delete the existing** `package.json`: Go ahead and delete the `package.json` file we created.
- **Navigate to the folder:** Open your terminal and navigate to the "my-custom-package" folder.
- **Run** `npm init`: Run the command `npm init`.

This will guide you through creating a `package.json` file. It will prompt you for values for various fields and try to guess sensible defaults. You can simply press enter to accept the defaults, or enter your own values.

Using `npm init -y` **for a quick setup**

If you're happy with the defaults and just want to quickly generate a `package.json` file, you can use the `-y` flag:

- **Delete the existing** `package.json`: Again, delete the existing file.
- **Run the command:** In your terminal, run `npm init -y`. This will create a `package.json` file with all the default values.

Understanding the generated `package.json`

You'll notice that your newly generated `package.json` file might have some extra fields that we didn't cover earlier. Don't worry, we'll explore those fields in future lessons. For now, just know that `package.json` is your go-to file for managing your Node.js package.

Now that we understand how to create and configure our `package.json` file, we're ready to learn how to install packages from the npm registry into our project!

Installing Packages

Let's say we need to take some text from our program and convert it to all uppercase letters. While we could do this using regular JavaScript code, we're going to use npm to show you how it works.

Finding the Right Tool
We need to find the perfect tool for the job. Head over to https://www.npmjs.com/ (the npm website). This is where you'll find all sorts of amazing packages. In the search bar, type in 'upper' (since we want to change text to uppercase). You'll see a bunch of options. Look for one called `upper-case`. This one seems like it will do what we need!

Evaluating Your Choice
- **Is it a good fit?** Before we install a tool, we need to make sure it's reliable. Here are a few things to look for:
  - **Published Date:** A newer date is usually better (but not always!). For simple tools like changing text to uppercase, a tool from a few years ago might still be fine.
  - **Downloads:** The more downloads a package has, the more likely it is to be stable and reliable. Millions of downloads are a good sign!
  - **Package Size:** Large packages can slow down your project. Look for smaller packages when possible. A few kilobytes is generally

no problem.

- **Documentation and Issues:** Make sure the package has good instructions and isn't riddled with bugs.

The `upper-case` package seems to check all the boxes, so let's install it!

Installing Your New Tool:

On the npm website, you'll see a command like this:

```
npm install upper-case
```

Copy that command. Now, open your VS Code project, open your terminal, and paste the command. Press enter! You'll see a progress bar as npm downloads the tool. It will be placed in a folder called `node_modules` in your project.

You'll also see two files get updated:

`package.json`: This file keeps track of all the tools you've installed. A new entry will be added for `upper-case`, along with the version you installed.

`package-lock.json`: This file helps make sure everyone on your team is using the same versions of all the tools.

Removing a Tool:

What if you need to remove a tool? No problem! Just use the following command in your terminal:

```
npm uninstall upper-case
```

This will remove the package from your project, `node_modules`, `package.json` and `package-lock.json`.

Using Packages

Remember, those packages we install are filled with code that we can use in our projects. Just like we used the `require` function to bring in built-in modules (like `fs` for working with files), we can use it to import our newly installed packages too.

Let's revisit our `uppercase` package. If we look at the package details on npmjs.com, we might find an example like this:

```
import { upperCase } from 'upper-case';
```

```
console.log(upperCase('hello world')); // HELLO WORLD
```

Let's break this down:

- `import {upperCase } from 'upper-case';`: This line brings in the `uppercase` function from our `uppercase` package. We're using `require('uppercase')` to access the package and then `.uppercase` to grab the specific function we want.
- `console.log(upperCase('Hello David'));`: Now we can use our `uppercase` function to transform our message to uppercase!

You should add `"type": "module",` to your package.json to treat your installed packages as Modules, or you change file extension to .mjs - index.mjs!

If we run this code using `node index.js`, we'll see the output:

```
HELLO David
```

And that's it! We successfully used a package installed from npm!

Now, let's say we needed to do something more complex, like copying an object in JavaScript. Instead of writing all that code ourselves, we can use a package called `lodash`! It's a giant toolbox of JavaScript tools, and it can handle all sorts of tasks like cloning objects.

This way, we can focus on building our project instead of re-inventing the wheel.

Managing Dependencies

In this lesson, we'll dive into the `dependencies` **field** in your `package.json` file. Think of it as a secret recipe for your Node.js project, telling everyone exactly what ingredients (packages) you need to make it work.

Remember how we installed the `uppercase` package in the previous lesson? Well, that's where this `dependencies` field comes into play. It keeps track of all the packages your project needs to run smoothly.

Imagine a real-life project where you have 5 to 50 different packages. You don't want to carry around a giant folder filled with all these packages (`node_modules`), especially when sharing your code with others! That's where version control comes in, but we need a way to tell our teammates what they need to download.

Let's see how this works in practice:

- **The** `node_modules` **Mystery:** Let's delete the `node_modules` folder in our project.

- **Running Our Code:** Now try running `node index.js`. You'll see an error like this:
- `Error: Cannot find module 'upper-case'`
- This means our project is missing the `uppercase` package!

- **Installing Dependencies:** To fix this, we can use the `npm install` command. This tells npm to look at our `package.json` file and install all the missing packages:
- `npm install`
- You'll see the `node_modules` folder magically reappear, containing all the necessary packages!

Now, if we run `node index.js` again, everything works as expected! We've successfully used `package.json` and `npm` to manage our project's dependencies.

Think of it like this:
- `package.json`: The shopping list for your Node.js project.
- `npm`: The grocery store where you get the ingredients.
- `node_modules`: The pantry where you store everything you bought.

Now you understand the importance of the `dependencies` field in `package.json` and how npm helps us manage our project's dependencies! This is a crucial step in making your Node.js projects more efficient and easier to share with others.

Versioning

In the previous lesson, we learned about the `dependencies` field in `package.json`. Each dependency is code that is needed for our project to work. Each entry lists the package name followed by the version installed. In this lesson, let's dive deeper into versioning in npm.

Let's say you want to install the latest version of a package called "uppercase." You can use the command `npm install uppercase`. This will always install the latest available version. But what if you want to install a specific version, like 2.0.0? You can do that by using the command `npm install uppercase@2.0.0`. This will overwrite the current version in your `package.json` file.

A common use case for installing a specific version is when the latest version has a bug that's been overlooked by the maintainers. You can install an earlier version, fix your project, and update to the latest version once the bug is patched. You can revert to the latest version by simply running `npm install uppercase`.

Now you might be wondering why the version numbers are represented as three digits separated by dots (like 2.0.2). Why not just use a simple sequential number like 1, 2, 3, and so on? That's because npm uses what's called **semantic versioning**. Let's break it down.

Semantic Versioning (SemVer) is a widely adopted system for assigning and incrementing version numbers. It's like a code language, making it clear what changes have been made to the code. SemVer uses a format like **x.y.z** where:

- **x** represents the **major version**.
- **y** represents the **minor version**.
- **z** represents the **patch version**.

For example, `uppercase` version `2.0.2` means:

- Major version: 2
- Minor version: 0
- Patch version: 2

Now, the big question: when do you bump each version number? You can't just randomly increase them, right? Here's the breakdown:

- **Patch version:** When you fix a bug and the code remains backwards compatible (meaning it doesn't break anything for users of older versions). For example, you might change 1.1.1 to 1.1.2.
- **Minor version:** When you add new functionality but the code stays backwards compatible. You also reset the patch version to zero. For example, you might change 1.1.1 to 1.2.0.
- **Major version:** When you make changes that break backwards

compatibility (meaning it won't work for users of older versions). You increment the major version and reset the minor and patch versions to zero. For example, you might change 1.1.1 to 2.0.0.

This semantic versioning system helps users make informed decisions about their projects.

A few more things about SemVer:

- Semantic versioning always starts with **0.1.0**. You never start with a patch version on a brand new package.
- A major version of 0 is used for initial development. Once the code is ready for production, you increment to version 1.0.0.
- **Every change**, even the simplest, should result in an increase in the version number.

Remember, as a developer, it's your responsibility to update the version number correctly based on the changes you make. As a user, it's your responsibility to stay aware of changes and make necessary updates to your project.

By understanding versioning and SemVer, you can navigate npm and ensure your projects are using the best and most reliable versions of packages.

Global Packages

Local packages are tools that are specific to a project. Global packages are tools that work on any project on your computer, not just one project.

One of the most popular global packages is **Nodemon**. It's a little helper that watches your code and automatically restarts your node.js app whenever you make changes. This saves you a ton of time because you don't have to manually restart the server each time you edit your code. Think of it as a super-fast code reloader!

To install Nodemon globally, we use this command in our terminal:

```
sudo npm install -g nodemon
```

The **-g** flag tells npm to install the package globally, making it accessible from any directory on your system. On Windows, you won't need to use `sudo to install it`.

Now, let's try it out. Let's say you have a file named `index.js` with this code:

```
console.log('Hello David! Welcome to David Mark!');
```

To run this with Nodemon, simply type:

```
nodemon index.js
```

You'll see the output in the terminal, and Nodemon will watch for changes in your `index.js` file. If you modify the code, for example, by adding an exclamation mark to the message:

```
console.log('Hello David! Welcome to David Mark!');
```

Save the file and watch as Nodemon restarts your app, displaying the updated output in the terminal.

Now, a quick note about global packages:

- They're not listed in your project's `package.json` file as dependencies.
- You need to install them globally for each developer on the team.

Global packages are like handy utilities for our Node.js projects. Think of them as power tools for development, helping you build amazing applications faster and more efficiently.

Exercise: Try installing and using another global package like or `prettier` (for code formatting).

Solution:

You can install `prettier` using the command `sudo npm install -g prettier`. Then, format your code with the command `prettier -- write filename.js`.

Scripts

Imagine you're working on a big project, and you need to run a buck of commands to build your application, start a development server, or maybe even format your code. It's a lot to remember, right? That's where npm scripts come in. You can define these commands once in your project's `package.json` file, and then everyone working on the project can use the same commands, ensuring consistency and making things a lot simpler.

So, how do you write these magical scripts? Well, they live within the `scripts` field of your `package.json` file. Let's take a look at an example:

```
{
  "name": "my-project",
  "version": "1.0.0",
  "description": "",
  "main": "index.js",
  "scripts": {
    "test": "echo \"Error: no test specified\" && exit 1"
  },
  "author": "",
  "license": "ISC"
}
```

See that `scripts` field? That's where we define our commands. We've got a "test" script here that doesn't do much, but it's a starting point.

Now, let's create a more useful script. Let's say we have a Node.js application running in a file named `index.js`. We can add a script to run this application:

```
{
  "name": "my-project",
  "version": "1.0.0",
  "description": "",
  "main": "index.js",
  "scripts": {
    "start": "node index.js"
  },
  "author": "",
  "license": "ISC"
}
```

We've added a `start` script that simply runs `node index.js`. Now, whenever you want to run your application, you just need to run `npm run start` in your terminal!

Let's break it down:

- `npm run`: This part tells npm that you want to execute a script.
- `start`: This is the name of the script we defined in our `package.json`.

Let's try it out! Open your terminal, navigate to your project directory, and run:

```
npm run start
```

If your `index.js` file prints something to the console, you should see that output in your terminal. It's that simple!

Remember: `start` is a special script. You can simply run `npm start` and it will automatically execute the `start` script defined in your `package.json`.

You'll find that npm scripts are a powerful tool that can streamline your development process. They're essential for any serious Node.js developer, so get familiar with them and start using them in your projects!

Publishing

We're going to publish a package to the npm registry, making it available for anyone to use. Now, this is where things get a bit more exciting.

First things first, you need an npm account. Head over to https://www.npmjs.com/ and click on "Sign up." Fill in the required info – username, email, and password. You'll receive a one-time password to your email, which you'll need to complete the signup process.

Now, open your terminal in VS Code and type in `npm adduser`. This will prompt you to enter your username, password, and email. These are the same ones you used to create your account on npmjs.com. Once you've done that, you're good to go!

To publish your package, use the command `npm publish`. If everything goes smoothly, you'll see your package on the npm registry at https://www.npmjs.com/package/. Look for the name you gave it in your `package.json` file.

Let's test this out. Create a new folder called `new-package` and navigate inside. Run `npm init -y` to create a basic `package.json` file. Now, let's install our published package using `npm install greet-david_mark`. This will add our package as a dependency to the project.

We'll create an `index.js` file and import our package:

```
import { greet } from 'greet-david_mark';

greet('David');
```

Now, run `node index.js`. The output should be `Hello David, welcome David Mark`. This demonstrates that you've successfully published your package and installed it in another project!

You've come a long way! We've covered the fundamental aspects of npm, including its role in managing dependencies, understanding `package.json`, installing and using packages, managing dependencies, global packages, creating npm scripts, and finally, publishing your own package.

Remember, this is just the tip of the iceberg! For a deeper dive into npm, head over to https://docs.npmjs.com/. It's packed with resources to help you master npm.

Building CLI Tools

In this lesson, we're building Command Line Interface (CLI) tools using Node.js and npm. CLI stands for Command Line Interface. Basically, it's a program you can run directly from your terminal. Think of popular CLIs like npm, which you've already encountered, or Git, which helps manage your code versions.

Our goal here is to create a simple CLI tool using Node.js. This lesson will focus on the basics of building a CLI, while the next lessons will explore passing options and adding interactivity. Let's get started!

Open your trusty VS Code and let's build our first CLI. Creating a CLI is very similar to creating an npm package, but with a few extra steps.

First, let's initialize a new npm project. Create a new folder called "my-custom-cli" and navigate to it in your terminal. Then, run the following command:

```
npm init -y
```

This will create a `package.json` file with default values.

Inside your `my-custom-cli` folder, open the `package.json` file and change the "name" to something unique, like "david_mark-nutshell".

Remember, npm doesn't allow duplicate package names, so make sure yours is original!

Now, let's write the code that will be executed when we run our CLI command. Create a new file named `index.js` inside the same folder and add a simple log statement:

```
console.log("David Mark nutshell");
```

The final step is to convert this package into a CLI. This requires two key additions:

- **Hashbang:** At the top of your `index.js` file, add the following line:

```
#!/usr/bin/env node
```

This line, known as a hashbang, tells the operating system which interpreter to use. In our case, we're specifying Node.js.

- **Bin Field:** Inside your `package.json` file, add a new field called "bin". This field allows you to treat your package as an executable file that can be installed into the system's PATH variable.

```
{
  "name": "david_mark-nutshell",
  "version": "1.0.0",
  "description": "",
  "main": "index.js",
  "scripts": {
    "test": "echo \"Error: no test specified\" && exit 1"
  },
  "author": "",
  "license": "ISC",
  "bin": {
    "cli-nutshell": "index.js"
  }
}
```

The `bin` field is an object where the key is the command you want to execute for your CLI (e.g., `cli-nutshell`) and the value is the entry point to your CLI (in this case, `index.js`).

And that's it! You've successfully created your first CLI tool.

To test it, we need to install our package globally. You might think we need to publish it first, but there's a quicker way. From within your project folder, run this command:

```
sudo npm install -g
```

Note that `sudo` is not required on Windows.

Running this command will install your CLI tool globally and register the command (`cli-nutshell`) in your system's PATH variable.

Now, open your terminal and run the command:

```
cli-nutshell
```

Press Enter, and you should see the output:

```
David Mark nutshell
```

That's our CLI working!

CLI Options

Let's add some logic and understand how to pass options to our CLI.

First, we need to write a function to print these moves. In our `index.js` file, let's create a function called `printUserInput`:

```
const printUserInput = async (userInput) => {
  console.log(userInput);
};
```

Now, we can call this function and pass in a user input:

```
printUserInput("Nutshell");
```

If you run `node index.js`, you'll see Nutshell printed in the terminal!

Making it Interactive

Currently, the user input is hardcoded. Let's make it dynamic so the user can enter any input!

We can use command-line arguments to pass the user input. In `index.js`, we can access these arguments using `process.argv`.

```
console.log(process.argv);
```

If you run `node index.js --user Nutshell`, you'll see an array of arguments in your console. The first two elements are the path to the Node interpreter and your `index.js` file. The remaining elements are the arguments you passed.

To handle these arguments more efficiently, we'll use a library called yargs. Let's install it using npm:

```
npm install yargs
```

Now, let's import and use yargs in our index.js file:

```
import yargs from 'yargs';
const argv = yargs(process.argv).argv;
```

We can now access the username option using argv.username:

```
printUserInput(argv.user);
```

Now, if you run node index.js --user Nutshell, you'll see Nutshell in your console! You can change the user input, and the CLI will update accordingly!

Interactive CLI Tools

In the last lesson, we learned how to make our CLI tool accept options from the command line. What if, instead of having users remember specific options, we could ask them directly what they want?

We're going to make our CLI interactive, prompting the user for a user input instead of requiring them to type it out as an option. It'll be much easier for anyone to use.

We'll add a new package called inquirer. This package will let us create interactive prompts in our CLI. Open your terminal and run this command:

```
npm install inquirer
```

Once inquirer is installed, you'll see it listed under your project's dependencies. Let's start using it! Open your index.js file and add these lines at the top:

```
import { inquirer } from 'inquirer';
```

Now, after the printUserInput function, we'll add the interactive prompt code. Let me guide you through it step-by-step:

First, we create a prompt module:

```
const prompt = inquirer.createPromptModule();
```

Then, we call this prompt function with an array of questions we want to ask the user. In this case, we just have one question:

```
prompt([
```

```
  {
    type: 'input',
    name: 'username',
    message: 'Enter your username:',
  },
]).then((answers) => {
  const username = answers.username;
  printUserInput(username);
});
```

In this code, we define the question as an object within the array. The `type` is set to `input`, indicating that we expect the user to enter text. The `name` is `username`, which we'll use to refer to the user's answer later. The `message` is what the user will see on the screen.

When the user enters their answer, it's returned to us in the `then` block. Inside the `then` block, we use an arrow function to receive the answers. We then extract the `username` value from the `answers` object. Finally, we call the `printUserInput` function, passing the user's chosen username as the argument.

That's it! Now, when you run `node index.js`, the CLI will prompt you to enter a user input. Try it out! Enter a user input, and you'll see the username displayed in the terminal.

Remember, we're just scratching the surface of what's possible with CLI tools and Node.js. There's so much more you can explore to build incredible tools that can help you in your daily workflow!

Cluster Module

Remember how we learned that Node.js is single-threaded? This means it only utilizes a single core of your CPU, regardless of how many cores your machine has. This is great for I/O operations, but if your code involves long-running, CPU-intensive tasks, your application might suffer from performance issues. To tackle this, Node.js introduced the `cluster` module.

The `cluster` module allows you to create child processes, known as workers, which run concurrently. These workers share the same server port. Essentially, the `cluster` module provides a quick and efficient way to handle workloads in your Node.js application. Let's understand this better with an example.

We'll start by creating a new file called `new_cluster.js`. We'll write a basic HTTP server that demonstrates the difference between using and not using the `cluster` module.

```
const http = require('http');
const server = http.createServer((req, res) => {
  if (req.url === '/') {
    res.writeHead(200, { 'Content-Type': 'text/plain' });
    res.end('Home Page');
  } else if (req.url === '/slow_page') {
    for (let i = 0; i < 10000000000000; i++) {
      // Simulating long-running CPU work
    }
    res.writeHead(200, { 'Content-Type': 'text/plain' });
    res.end('Slow Page');
  }
});

server.listen(8000, () => {
  console.log('Server is running on port 8000');
});
```

This simple server has two routes:

- '/': Responds with "Home Page" quickly.
- '/**slow_page**': Has a long-running `for` loop that simulates intensive CPU work, making it take significantly longer to respond.

Now, let's run this code with `node new_cluster.js`. You'll see the server running on port 8000. In your browser, navigate to `http://localhost:8000`. You'll see the "Home Page".

Next, open the network tab in your browser's developer tools. Reload the page. You'll likely see the Home Page load in just a few milliseconds. Now, open a new tab, go to the network tab, and navigate to `http://localhost:8000/slow_page`. This will take considerably longer, perhaps a few seconds. This is expected because of the simulated CPU-intensive work.

Here's the interesting part: Load the `slow_page` first. While it's loading, quickly open a new tab, go to the network tab, and navigate to the home page. Reload the home page. Notice what happens: the `slow_page` is loading, the home page keeps loading too!

Why is this? Remember, Node.js is single-threaded. The `slow_page` is blocking the server's single thread, preventing it from responding to other requests.

To fix this blocking issue, we'll use the `cluster` module. Let's understand how it works first.

Imagine you run `node index.js`. This file becomes the "cluster master". The master's job is to spawn new "workers", each running an instance of your Node.js application. The master itself doesn't handle requests, read files, or do other application tasks. It's only responsible for managing the workers - starting, stopping, restarting, etc.

Each worker has its own event loop, memory, and V8 instance. This allows us to distribute the workload across multiple instances without blocking incoming requests.

Let's modify our code to use the `cluster` module. We'll create a new file called `cluster.js`.

```js
const cluster = require('cluster');
const http = require('http');

if (cluster.isMaster) {
  console.log(`Master process ${process.pid} is
running`);

  // Create 2 worker processes
  for (let i = 0; i < 2; i++) {
    cluster.fork();
  }

  cluster.on('exit', (worker, code, signal) => {
    console.log(`worker ${worker.process.pid} died`);
  });
} else {
  console.log(`Worker process ${process.pid} started`);

  const server = http.createServer((req, res) => {
    if (req.url === '/') {
      res.writeHead(200, { 'Content-Type':
'text/plain' });
      res.end('Home Page');
    } else if (req.url === '/slow_page') {
      for (let i = 0; i < 1000000000000; i++) {
```

```
        // Simulating long-running CPU work
      }
      res.writeHead(200, { 'Content-Type':
'text/plain' });
      res.end('Slow Page');
    }
  });

  server.listen(8000, () => {
    console.log('Server is running on port 8000');
  });
}
```

In this code:

- `cluster.isMaster`: This checks if the current process is the master. If it is, we print a message and create two workers using `cluster.fork()`.
- `cluster.on('exit', ...)`: This event listener is triggered when a worker process exits.
- **If not the master**: We run the same server code as before.

Now, run `node cluster.js`. You should see messages indicating the master and two workers are running. Go back to your browser, reload the home page, and then quickly reload the slow page. You'll likely see the home page load instantly, while the `slow_page` takes a bit longer.

Why does this work? The master process has spawned two worker processes. The first request to `slow_page` is handled by one worker, while the home page request is handled by the other worker. This means the `slow_page` request no longer blocks the home page request.

Important: Create at least two workers. Creating only one worker essentially replicates the single-threaded behavior, as you still have just one instance of your Node.js application handling requests.

You might be tempted to create a large number of workers to boost performance. However, that's not always the case. Ideally, you should create only as many workers as there are CPU cores on your machine. Creating more workers than cores can actually lead to performance degradation as the system has to manage more processes with fewer available cores.

To find out how many CPU cores your machine has, you can use the `os`

module:
```
const os = require('os');
console.log(os.cpus().length);
```
Running this code will tell you the number of logical cores on your machine.

But there's an easier way to manage all of this: using the `pm2` package. `pm2` is a process manager that can help you run your application as a cluster and automatically determine the optimal number of workers. Install `pm2` globally using:
```
sudo npm install -g pm2
```
(You might need to use `npm` instead of `sudo npm` on Windows.)

Now, you can use `pm2` to run your `cluster.js` file in cluster mode:
```
pm2 start cluster.js -i 0
```
The `-i 0` tells `pm2` to determine the optimal number of workers to create based on your system's CPU cores.

You'll see a table in your terminal displaying the running workers. You can then test your home page and slow page requests again, and you should see similar performance improvements as before.

To stop `pm2`, run:
```
pm2 stop cluster.js
```
That's a lot to take in about the `cluster` module, but hopefully, it all makes sense. This is a valuable concept to know about even if you're a beginner, although it's not something you'll use right away.

Make sure to explore the `pm2` package further! It's a powerful tool that can help you manage your Node.js applications effectively.

Worker Threads Module

In the last lesson, we talked about the **Cluster Module**, which is a powerful tool for boosting performance in Node.js applications. Now, we'll explore the **Worker Threads Module**, another performance-enhancing gem that works hand-in-hand with Node.js.

Imagine you're running a restaurant. You have a lot of customers, and you want to serve them all quickly. The **Cluster Module** is like hiring more cooks to handle the orders. Each cook can process a customer's order independently, leading to faster service. However, what if you need to make a special dish that takes a long time to prepare? This is where the **Worker Threads Module** comes in handy. It's like having a separate kitchen for those complex dishes. The main kitchen continues to handle the regular orders while the specialized kitchen tackles the time-consuming one, all without slowing down the main restaurant.

Let's break it down further. The **Worker Threads Module** allows you to create **threads** within your Node.js application. These threads run in **separate processes**, independent of the main application. Think of it as having multiple small engines working simultaneously within a single car. This prevents long-running tasks from blocking the main application's ability to handle other requests.

So how is this different from the **Cluster Module**? Well, the **Cluster Module** creates multiple copies of your Node.js application, each with its own event loop and memory. The **Worker Threads Module**, on the other hand, stays within a single Node.js instance, using separate threads.

Let's dive into some code and see how it all works.

First, create a file called `main-thread.js`. This file will hold our main application code.

```
const http = require('http');
const { Worker } = require('worker_threads');

const server = http.createServer((req, res) => {
  if (req.url === '/') {
    res.end('<h1>Home</h1>');
  } else if (req.url === '/slow-page') {
    let j = 0;
    const worker = new Worker('./worker-thread.js');
    worker.on('message', (data) => {
      res.end(`<h1>Slow Page - J: ${data}</h1>`);
    });
    worker.postMessage(j);
  }
});

server.listen(8000, () => {
```

```
  console.log('Server listening on port 8000');
});
```

Now, let's create a second file named `worker-thread.js`. This file will hold the code for our worker thread.

```
const { parentPort } = require('worker_threads');

parentPort.on('message', (j) => {
  for (let i = 0; i < 1000000000; i++) {
    j++;
  }
  parentPort.postMessage(j);
});
```

Let's break down the code:

- In `main-thread.js`, we import the `http` module for creating a server and the `Worker` class from the `worker_threads` module.

- We handle two routes: `/` and `/slow-page`. The `/slow-page` route simulates a long-running task by incrementing a variable `j` within a loop.

- For the `/slow-page` route, we create a new worker thread using the `Worker` class and pass the path to the `worker-thread.js` file as an argument.

- We use `worker.postMessage(j)` to send the value of `j` to the worker thread.

- We listen for messages from the worker thread using `worker.on('message', (data) => {...})`. This callback function receives the data sent back by the worker thread and responds with the data.

- In `worker-thread.js`, we import the `parentPort` object, which allows communication back to the main thread.

- We listen for messages from the main thread using `parentPort.on('message', (j) => {...})`.

- Within the callback function, we receive the `j` value, perform our long-running task (incrementing `j`), and then send the updated `j` back to the main thread using `parentPort.postMessage(j)`.

Now, run the `main-thread.js` file using `node main-thread.js` in your terminal. Then, open your browser and visit `http://localhost:8000/`. The home page should load quickly. Now, go to `http://localhost:8000/slow-page`. You'll see that the page takes a few seconds to load, but the home page continues to respond quickly. This demonstrates that the long-running task is being executed in a separate thread without blocking the main thread.

The **Worker Threads Module** is a powerful tool for improving performance in Node.js applications, especially when dealing with long-running tasks. It's like having a team of helpers working behind the scenes to keep things running smoothly.

Remember, this is just a brief introduction. The **Worker Threads Module** has a lot more to offer. For deeper exploration, check out the official Node.js documentation.

Exercise:

Try modifying the code to send a message with the current time from the main thread to the worker thread, and then have the worker thread print this time to the console.

Solution:

```
// main-thread.js
const http = require('http');
const { Worker } = require('worker_threads');

const server = http.createServer((req, res) => {
  if (req.url === '/') {
    res.end('<h1>Home</h1>');
  } else if (req.url === '/slow-page') {
    const now = new Date();
    const worker = new Worker('./worker-thread.js');
    worker.on('message', (data) => {
      res.end(`<h1>Slow Page - Time: ${data}</h1>`);
    });
    worker.postMessage(now);
  }
});

server.listen(8000, () => {
  console.log('Server listening on port 8000');
});
```

```
// worker-thread.js
const { parentPort } = require('worker_threads');

parentPort.on('message', (time) => {
  console.log(`Time from main thread: ${time}`);
});
```

This will send the current time from the main thread to the worker thread, which will then print it to the console.

Deploying Your Node.js App

In this lesson, we're going to learn how to take our Node.js application and make it accessible to the world! There are a lot of cool ways to do this, but we'll be focusing on using a platform called **Render**.

First, we need to make sure our code is ready for deployment. In this example, we'll use a simple **index.js** file that sets up a basic HTTP server. It will respond with a "Hello World!" message when you visit the website. Here's what it looks like:

```
const http = require('http');

const port = process.env.PORT || 3000;

const server = http.createServer((req, res) => {
  res.writeHead(200, { 'Content-Type': 'text/plain' });
  res.end('Hello World!\n');
});

server.listen(port, () => {
  console.log(`Server running on port ${port}`);
});
```

Important Note: This code utilizes the `process.env.PORT` variable to make our app more flexible. We'll see how to use this later on!

Step 1: GitHub

Before deploying, it's a good practice to store your code on GitHub. Think of it as a safe and organized place for your project files.

Step 2: Render

Head over to render.com and create a free account. Render makes deploying your Node.js applications super easy!

Step 3: Linking Your GitHub Account

Once you're signed in, you'll see your dashboard. To start the deployment process, click on the "New Web Service" button. You'll be asked to connect your GitHub account. Enter your credentials, and give Render permission to access the repositories you want to deploy.

Step 4: Setting Up Your Deployment

Now, click on "New Web Service" again. This time, choose the repository containing your Node.js code. You'll need to enter a few details:

- **Service Name:** Give your deployment a name. For example, "NodeJS-App-1".
- **Region:** This determines where your server will be located. You can leave it as the default for now.
- **Branch:** Select the branch you want to deploy.
- **Root Directory:** Point to the folder containing your **index.js** file.
- **Build Command:** If your project has a `package.json` file, you might need a command to build your application. We'll leave it empty for now.
- **Start Command:** This tells Render how to start your Node.js application. Here, it would be `node index.js`.
- **Environment Variables:** Remember the `process.env.PORT` variable in our code? We need to define it here! Set the key to `PORT` and the value to 80.

Click on "Create Web Service". Render will start deploying your app, and you'll see a status indicating progress.

Step 5: Your App is Live!

Once the deployment is complete, you should see a link to your app! Clicking on this link will open a new tab, and you should see your "Hello World!" message.

Congratulations! You've just deployed your first Node.js application.

What is next

First, I highly recommend exploring **Express.js**. It's a web framework built on top of Node.js, making it super easy to build robust web applications. You can think of Express.js as a powerful engine that makes building APIs a breeze.

Next, consider learning about **Jest** or **Mocha**, powerful testing frameworks. They'll help you write tests for your Node.js applications, ensuring your code behaves as expected and catches any bugs early on.

Finally, **TypeScript** is a great addition to your Node.js arsenal. It adds types to your code, catching errors early and making your code more readable and maintainable. Think of it as adding extra safety and structure to your Node.js programs.